# Oldest
# St. Louis

### NINI HARRIS

REEDY PRESS

We (the publisher and the author) have done our best to provide the most accurate information available when this book was completed. However, we make no warranty, guarantee, or promise about the accuracy, completeness, or currency of the information provided, and we expressly disclaim all warranties, expressed or implied. Please note that attractions, company names, addresses, websites, and phone numbers are subject to change or closure, and this is outside of our control. We are not responsible for any loss, damage, injury, or inconvenience that may occur due to the use of this book.

Library of Congress Control Number: 2020938243

ISBN: 9781681062792

Cover Design: Jill Halpin
Book Design: Linda Eckels

Cover photo credit, clockwise from top left: St. Louis University High School, courtesy of NiNi Harris; the Fox Theatre Organ in 1929, courtesy of the Missouri Historical Society; the Muny Opera Box Office, courtesy of the Muny; the Soulard Spice Shop, courtesy of Linda Schmitz.

Printed in the United States of America
20 21 22 23 24    5 4 3 2 1

# TABLE OF CONTENTS

## SOUTH

# WEST

# ACKNOWLEDGMENTS

Special thanks to John Waide, Archivist Emeritus, Pius XII Memorial Library at Saint Louis University. John generously shared his extraordinary skills at locating primary source materials at a time when a pandemic had closed many libraries and archives. His contributions were critical to this project.

The following individuals helped locate and access historical materials:

St. Louis Public Library staff members Adele Heagney and Kirwin Roach in the St. Louis Room and Renee Jones in Special Collections.

Andy Hahn, director of the Campbell House Museum.

Andrew Schleicher, archives technician at the Carondelet Historical Society.

Catherine Lucy, Director of Carondelet Consolidated Archive, Sisters of St. Joseph of Carondelet.

Lynn Marie Alexander, director/archivist, Hill Neighborhood Center.

Carolyn (Ranzini) Stelzer of the Hill.

Lynn Segura of the Office of Consecrated Life, St. Louis Archdiocese.

Rena Schergen and Sarah Coffey of the St. Louis Archdiocesan Archives.

Catherine Martin, public information officer, Missouri Botanical Garden.

Lauren Sallwasser, associate archivist, and Jason Stratman, assistant librarian, Missouri Historical Society.

Steve Butz, Missouri State Representative of the 81st House District.

Laura Peters, archivist at The Municipal Opera Association.

Stuart Baker, supervisor, and Jevons Brown, clerk, Records Retention, Comptrollers Office, City of St. Louis.

Bette Constantin, Ann Greenstein, Esley Hamilton, Amanda McMichael, Emma Prince, and Marilyn Telowitz provided editorial input.

# INTRODUCTION

St. Louis is more than just the metro economy, or the current-day population, or the landscape of suburban municipalities connected by interstates with a historic city. It is a series of collective memories and experiences that grow from the fabric of St. Louis. That collective memory is made up of fragrances, sounds, streetscapes, flavors, and historic architecture. The fabric, or civic stage, for those experiences are our oldest businesses, institutions, and urban landscapes.

*Oldest St. Louis* explores the story and character of the city's most long-lived landmarks and experiences: the park with sheltering trees and delightful landscapes that has enriched the life of St. Louisans for over 180 years; the neighborhood diner that for a half-century has served old-fashioned country cooking and soul food like grandma—who came North during the great migration—used to make for Sunday dinners; the spectacular shows with lots of scenery, song, and dance produced under the stars at the Muny for a hundred seasons; the flavor of golden pretzels warm from the oven and baked as they have been for a century; attending a wedding at a stone church on the riverfront that witnessed the levee lined with paddle wheelers and soldiers heading to Civil War battles; and standing in a line outside a 19th-century building waiting for a BLT and a thick malt.

*Oldest St. Louis* traces the stories of gifts from our civic ancestors—extraordinary architecture, museums, schools, and libraries—that punctuate the landscapes of 21st-century lives and experiences. It looks at some of the oldest family businesses that have carried on traditions, skills, and crafts for generations. These businesses reflect St. Louis's rich ethnic heritage while supporting families and building the community's economic resilience.

Some of the oldest places and businesses featured in *Oldest St. Louis* are little nuggets of sweetness left over from an era when Americans spent Friday nights at the bowling alley, or swing dancing at a ballroom, or hanging out at a neighborhood tavern. Others have enhanced the lives of citizens in unique ways, like the annual orchid show at the Botanical Garden or the 15th-century book at the St. Louis Public Library.

Many of the stories told here are inspiring: the congregation founded and nurtured by a man born into slavery; the man who started as a clerk, made a fortune, and then left it to build Barnes Hospital; and the kosher butcher shop that was started by Holocaust survivors.

These simple stories are more than just local trivia. The histories of these landmarks help preserve the triumphs of individual St. Louisans, recall the little joys that enriched lives, and contribute to the very character of the St. Louis community and the framework for its future.

# Downtown &
# Grand Center

## 1474

# OLDEST LIBRARY BOOK

## A TIE:
### SMALL BUNDLES OF TIME
St. Louis Public Library, 1300 Olive St.

### BOOK OF RURAL BENEFITS
Missouri Botanical Garden Library

The oldest books in St. Louis libraries date to within a few decades of Johannes Gutenberg introducing his printing press. After a decade of experimentation, Gutenberg devised a press with movable metal type. By 1452, he had begun his famous Bible project, printing about 200 beautiful bibles. His less-costly means of reproducing the written word would spread literacy, help build a middle class, and even spur a religious reformation across Europe. The two oldest library books in St. Louis libraries date to 1474, only 22 years after Gutenberg started printing his bibles.

The St. Louis Public Library's copy of *Fasciculus Temporum* (or *Small Bundles of Time)* is from the first printing of this 15th-century bestseller. An illustrated history of the world from creation to the time of Pope Sixtus IV, it was written by a Carthusian monk in Cologne. The monk, Werner Rolewinck (1425–1502), wrote *Small Bundles of Time* in Latin, the language of the Roman Catholic Church. Arnold Ther Hoerner, also of Cologne, issued this first edition, which is illustrated with hand-colored woodcuts. During the 15th century, 33 editions and translations of this world history were published.

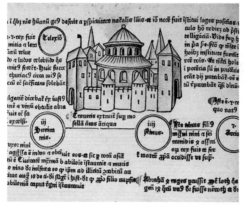

Colorized wood cuts (one showing a walled medieval city) illustrate a history of the world published in 1474. Fasciculus Temporum, *which measures 11.5 inches long by 8.5 inches wide, is the oldest book in the collections of St. Louis Public Library. (Photo courtesy of St. Louis Public Library.)*

The Missouri Botanical Garden Library includes a copy of *Opus Ruralium Commodorum,* or *The Book of Rural Benefits,* also printed in 1474. This was the first printed text on agriculture and was based on classical and medieval sources. It was the work of Pietro de' Crescenzi of Bologna. De' Crescenzi worked as a lawyer and a judge. After his retirement, he divided his time between Bologna and his country estate outside the city walls. Life at his estate likely inspired *Opus Ruralium Commodorum,* which he had completed by 1309.

Numerous manuscript copies of de Crescenzi's work circulated before it was first published by Johann Schussler in Augsburg in 1471. During the 16th century, 57 editions were published in Latin, Italian, French, German, and Polish.

---

A German surgical text by Ortolf von Bayrlandt, published in 1477, is in the collections of the Bernard Becker Medical Library, which serves the Washington University Medical Center. Established in 1911, the library is one of the oldest and most comprehensive medical libraries west of the Mississippi.

---

# Oldest Church
## The Old Cathedral
### Gateway Arch National Park

T he stone Old Cathedral looks almost quaint as it sits in the expansive lawns in the shadow of the soaring, stainless steel Gateway Arch. When this Cathedral was dedicated, however, its scale seemed impressive and its classical style announced that St. Louis was becoming a sophisticated metropolis.

The site of the Old Cathedral was set aside for a church by Pierre Laclede when he founded St. Louis in 1764. Three churches were constructed on the site before the Old Cathedral was built. The first church was a small cabin built in 1770. Six years later, it was replaced by a second larger log church. Then a larger brick church was begun in 1818.

In 1834, when the Old Cathedral was dedicated, French log houses still dotted the riverfront, in between the then-new brick houses, stores, and warehouses. Paddle wheelers, belching smoke, lined the levee. Roustabouts hauled crates and barrels up and down the gang planks. Above this bustling scene rose the spire of the stone, Greek Revival-style cathedral topped by a gold gilt cross.

The scale of the polished stone cathedral seemed dramatic—136 feet long and 84 feet wide. The facade stood 50 feet tall, and the spire rested upon a 40-foot stone tower.

Not just its scale, but the cathedral's dignified Greek Revival style reflected the beginnings of refinement in frontier St. Louis. Its 40-foot-wide portico rested on four Doric columns. The

*When completed in 1834, the Cathedral cost $63,360 to build. (Postcard courtesy of NiNi Harris.)*

cathedral was described as a "noble edifice," and admired for its "general beauty and symmetry."[1]

During the nearly two centuries following the dedication of the Old Cathedral, its setting has gone through radical changes. In 1849, a fire devastated the riverfront, remarkably sparing the Cathedral. When the riverfront was rebuilt, the large warehouses dwarfed the Old Cathedral. After railroads carried commerce away from the riverfront, the area became dismal. Later, the riverfront warehouses were razed to create the setting for the Gateway Arch. Today the Old Cathedral is an active Roman Catholic parish, surrounded by a national park.

---

*Holy Family Church in nearby Cahokia, Illinois, built in 1799 of French-style, vertical log construction, is probably the oldest church in the Mississippi Valley.*

---

# ─1912

# OLDEST CONCERT HALL
## THE SHELDON
3648 Washington Ave.

Whether a trio is singing Irish ballads or a string quartet is performing Bach, the Sheldon Concert Hall at the heart of Grand Center provides a remarkable environment in which to appreciate the music. Though the Sheldon was built by the Ethical Society and its auditorium was designed to host lectures, it also has exceptional acoustics for musical performances.

The Ethical Society of Saint Louis, a Humanist congregation founded in 1886, built the Sheldon as their home in 1912. Architect Louis Spiering designed the Classical Revival building—of brown brick with a two-story Ionic porch and decorative front panels of Bedford stone—for the Ethical Society.

Spiering, a German American professor of architecture, worked with acoustical engineers to design the Society's 712-seat auditorium. He designed the auditorium to have no 90-degree angles. Empty spaces allowed the sound to travel. The wood from fir trees was chosen for the seats, because that wood absorbs and reflects just the right amount of sound. Empty space and a mound of dirt beneath the stage helped the sound resonate.

Speakers who have appeared at the auditorium include Albert Einstein, Ernest Hemingway, Dwight Eisenhower, Thurgood Marshall, and Margaret Mead.

In 1964, a time when offices and theatre audiences were abandoning Grand Center, the Ethical Society built a new home in

*Artist F. Humphrey Woolrych created this architectural rendering of The Sheldon. (Photo courtesy of Missouri Historical Society.)*

St. Louis County. During the next quarter-century, benign neglect took its toll on the extraordinary concert hall in Grand Center.

In 1988, the nonprofit Sheldon Arts Foundation was formed and three years later it purchased the facility to preserve it as one of St. Louis's important cultural resources. In 1998, the former home of the Ethical Society was restored and reopened as The Sheldon. (It was named for Walter L. Sheldon, the first leader of the Ethical Society in St. Louis.) The $5 million project restored the historic structure with its spectacular auditorium and upstairs ballroom and added elevators, meeting space, and exhibit galleries. Since its renovation and expansion, The Sheldon has welcomed hundreds of events each year, featuring both local artists and the world's finest musicians performing jazz, folk, and classical music.

---

*Architect Louis Clemens Spiering never saw his premier work, The Sheldon. He died at the age of 37, months before its completion.*

---

# OLDEST HOUSE GARDEN
## THE CAMPBELL HOUSE GARDEN

1508 Locust St.

Downtown St. Louis boasts 91 landscaped acres surrounding the Gateway Arch and a ribbon of parkway stretching from the Old Courthouse to Union Station. During the 19th and early 20th centuries, however, all these blocks of parkland were covered with buildings. Only one landscaped corner in downtown has always been a garden: the garden of the Robert Campbell House. It is also documented that the garden of the Campbell House has been cultivated every season since 1856.

This land was still grazing land when it was platted as Lucas Place, an elegant residential district on what were at the time the western outskirts of St. Louis. The tall, narrow townhouse at 1508 Lucas Place (now Locust Street) was built in 1851. The handsome brick house originally sat on a 40-foot-wide lot. In

1854, Robert Campbell, one of the most successful businessmen on the American frontier, bought the house.

On January 7, 1856, Campbell purchased the adjacent and

*The garden of the Robert Campbell House Museum features the original, 19th century lattice-work gazebo. (Photo courtesy of the Robert Campbell House Museum.)*

still-vacant corner lot. The price tag—$8,100—attests to the exclusivity of the new subdivision. The lot measured 50 feet wide and 155 feet deep, considerable space for a garden. Even though the garden was at the corner, it offered seclusion. The Campbell family lined the garden's 15th Street side with a seven-foot-tall board fence. A cast-iron fence sat atop a stone ledge facing Lucas Place. There were trellises and a lattice-work gazebo that stretched across the width of the garden. Nineteenth-century photos show it was lush with plantings and trees.

The townhouse at 1508 Lucas Place was home to members of the Campbell family until 1938. Five years later, civic-minded St. Louisans opened the house as a museum, featuring the family's personal furnishings. Throughout the decades, the museum staff and volunteers have maintained the Victorian-era urban garden with its delightful gazebo and ornamental iron fence and replicated the 19th-century birdhouse. The old-fashioned, terraced garden is planted with irises, day lilies, peonies, and roses. Geraniums and marigolds add summer color. Akebia, a trailing, flowering vine, drapes over the gazebo.

While the Campbell family enjoyed the privacy of their outdoor haven, today the 164-year-old garden hosts parties for museum members and, in conjunction with the Union Avenue Opera, the annual garden concert, "Arias in the Afternoon."

---

*Architect Thomas Warying Walsh, in partnership with Joseph Edgar, designed the Campbell House. Later in his career, Walsh would design St. Francis Xavier Church (The College Church) at Grand and Lindell Boulevards.*

---

# Oldest Hotel
## The Marriott Grand
800 Washington Ave.

Historic buildings that were constructed as office buildings, banks, a shoe factory, and a YMCA have been converted into unique hotels. In an era of chain motels and superhighway travel, these transformed buildings make attractive and appealing hotels. Though they date to the 1890s and the turn of the 20th century, St. Louis's oldest hotel that was originally built as a hotel is the Marriott Grand, constructed in 1917.

The Marriott Grand's Crystal Ballroom offers dramatic views of downtown St. Louis. This red brick, 23-story hotel on Washington Avenue is also a landmark in the St. Louis skyline. Its top two stories, faced with limestone, form an Ionic colonnade crowned with a bracketed cornice. The hotel's first three floors are also stone-faced and are punctuated by great arched windows. Restrained and classically inspired, it was recognized by the Art League as the best building constructed in St. Louis in 1917.

*This early postcard promoting the elegant Statler Hotel boasted that the hotel not only had 650 rooms, but 650 baths too, making it one of the "most modern Hotels in the down-town district." (Postcard courtesy of NiNi Harris.)*

The 650-room hotel boasted two opulent public spaces: the hotel's ballroom and the original lobby. The ceiling of the hotel's two-story lobby, now an event space, forms vaults. Its delicate plasterwork features classical designs with Wedgewood-like medallions in pale blue. The scale of the Crystal Ballroom, 43 by 116 feet, is dramatic. Two-story Corinthian piers frame the huge windows that line the ballroom.

The hotel was built as the fourth hotel in the Statler chain. Its glamorous design was the work of the influential New York firm of Post & Sons with St. Louis's Mauran, Russell, and Crowell.

Conrad Hilton bought the Statler Hotels in 1954, and the Washington Avenue hotel became The Statler Hilton St. Louis. Its prestige had already faded before it was renamed the Gateway Hotel and it was bought by Denver businessman Victor Sayyah and St. Louis political powerhouse Peter J. Webbe in 1981. The once-elegant hotel became known for its bargain-basement rates. The hotel's future was already in question by February 12, 1987, when a fire mysteriously started on three floors of the hotel simultaneously. The damaged hotel sat empty for years before a renovation in 2002 expanded the hotel and restored its facades, its spectacular lobby, and its ballroom.

---

*When Union Station opened in 1894, its headhouse included the Terminal Hotel. Its 75 small rooms were furnished only with a bed and washstand. The plumbing consisted of a water pitcher and bowl to wash up. As part of the 1985 renovation of Union Station, a new hotel wing was built underneath the train shed.*

---

# 1862

# OLDEST MURALS
## THE CARL WIMAR MURALS IN THE OLD COURTHOUSE
4th St. at Market

The first murals painted west of the Mississippi were commissioned to decorate the interior of the rotunda of the then-new courthouse.

When the iron-framed dome of the Old Courthouse was completed in 1862, it dominated the St. Louis skyline. The Greek Revival-style courthouse, topped by a Renaissance-style dome, greeted river travelers arriving in St. Louis and "set a standard for other government buildings throughout the land," according to the National Park Service.[2]

The interior of the courthouse was equally dramatic. The 60-foot rotunda rose in four levels to the dome. Ornamental galleries with elegant balustrades circled the rotunda. The galleries rested on Ionic Greek columns. Though this remarkable courthouse had already required 23 years to complete, its decoration was only beginning. The panels and lunettes in the rotunda were waiting to be filled with murals.

German American artists August Becker and his half-brother, the principal artist, Carl Wimar (1828–1862), were commissioned to paint a series of frescoes in the rotunda. The American frontier had fascinated Wimar since he first came to St. Louis in 1844. After apprenticing with a local artist and decorator, he returned to Germany to study art for four years in

*August Becker created this painting after the mural depicting the "founding of St. Louis" by his half brother, Carl Wimar. Becker assisted Wimar with his murals in the Old Courthouse. (Photo courtesy of Missouri Historical Society.)*

Dusseldorf. Once back in St. Louis, Wimar used his adopted city as his base to explore and paint images of the American frontier. His work provides insights into the American West—both its reality and its romance. In the courthouse, he painted historical vignette murals in four oval-shaped lunettes. The murals portray events in St. Louis history, including *The Founding of St. Louis: Pierre Laclede Coming Ashore* and *The Indians Attacking the Village of St. Louis, 1780.*

Originally, there were more than the four remaining frescoes by Wimar in the Old Courthouse, which he completed shortly before he passed away in November 1862. In 1880, however, artist Ettore Miragoli was commissioned to conserve the murals done by Wimar and paint additional murals in the rotunda. The Italian artist did not respect American artists nor, evidently, German American artists. Instead of conserving all of Wimar's original murals, he painted over some of them.

---

*When artist Carl Wimar was painting the frescoes in the Old Courthouse, he was so weakened from tuberculosis that he had to be carried to the top of the dome to do his work.*

---

# OLDEST PET FOOD
## PURINA DOG CHOW
801 Chouteau Ave.

When Ralston Purina began producing dog food in 1926, company founder William H. Danforth used the word "chow" for the name. During World War I, American doughboys had used the word "chow" as slang for Army food. While volunteering with servicemen in Europe, Danforth first heard the slang word and had been taken by it.

Later, he adopted the term for other products. Eventually Purina's offerings included hog chow, cattle chow, and horse chow. When NASA shot the first chimpanzee into space, he was fed Purina monkey chow. In 1963, Ralston Purina began producing Cat Chow for the nation's growing population of house cats.

At the same that Danforth introduced Dog Chow, the company established the first pet nutrition and care center at Purina Farms near Gray Summit, Missouri. At Purina Farms, staff tested their pet foods for nutritional value and to make sure the animals would find them tasty. When Admiral Richard E. Byrd searched for nutritional feed for his sled dogs for their two-year expedition to Antarctica in 1933, he chose Purina Dog Chow. His dogs ate tons of Dog Chow and thrived despite the harsh conditions.

Though Purina is known to most Americans for its line of pet foods (and is remembered for its cereals that are now produced by General Mills), the company originated with an effort to create better horse and mule feed.

Danforth, whose vision and hard work made Ralston Purina an industry giant, was the son of a merchant and farmer in Charleston, Missouri. When he graduated from Washington University in 1892 with a degree in engineering, he considered his father's advice to "get a universal business, one that meets people's needs regardless of seasons or depressions."[3] Danforth thought about the brick business, but he felt it was too seasonal. Instead, he entered the feed business, borrowing $4,000 from his father to buy a one-third interest in a feed store on Washington Avenue with a mill on 8th and Gratiot (the current corporate campus). At that time, there were only two kinds of feed for horses and mules: corn and oats. If the corn was poorly prepared,

Air View of The Purina Mills Plant at St. Louis, Mo.

*Postcard showing the old Ralston Purina complex at Gratiot and 8th Streets. The current, modern-style headquarters (Checkerboard Square) was built in 1968. (Postcard courtesy of NiNi Harris.)*

it could cause fatal colic in the animals. Though oats were much safer, they were also much costlier.

By mixing the two feeds, Danforth created a very marketable product. He sold it with the slogan "Cheaper than oats and safer than corn." He mixed the first bags of mule feed by hand on the floor of a mill. For the name of his company, he chose a combination of Ralston, the name of a national health club, and Purina, meaning purity.

Danforth was looking for a gimmick to make Ralston Purina's animal feed stand out. He recalled a family that had come to his father's general store in Charleston, when Danforth was a boy. The entire family was wearing clothing made by hand of fabric with a checkerboard pattern. Remembering how distinctive the pattern was, in 1902 Danforth adopted the checkerboard design for his feed bags. Soon the bold red and white checkerboard appeared on silos and feed stores all over the nation. The checkerboard appeared on the company's breakfast cereals. It also became Danforth's personal signature. He wore checkerboard ties and shirts, and checkerboard coats.[4]

---

*William Danforth encouraged Ralston Purina*
*employees and their families to sing the company song,*
*"Fight, Fight, Fight for Old Purina."*
  *"Fight, fight, fight for old Purina.*
  *There's a chow for every need.*
  *Never let the battle stop.*
  *Keep the Checkerboard on top.*
  *Fight to keep good old Purina in the lead."*

---

# OLDEST RADIO STATION
## WEW AM 770

Bosnian music, conversation and commentary fill the airwaves from noon to sign-off each weekday on WEW Radio. Saturday programing, beginning at noon, is Hispanic themed. WEW's Sunday schedule includes the Croatian Hour, the Italian Hour, German Talk Radio, and the Polish Polka Program. Known for decades as the station that celebrates St. Louis's immigrant communities, the origins of WEW can be traced to a Jesuit Brother with Saint Louis University during the early days of wireless transmission.

In 1912, Brother George Rueppel started using the university's new wireless station to send out weather reports in Morse code to train stations and farm bureaus around the country. Farmers would gather at these stations to hear the telegraph operators read Rueppel's reports to them. Brother Rueppel and the Science Division had earned a license to operate a "Technical and Training School" station by early 1915. WEW's inaugural broadcast of actual voices, not Morse code, was on April 21, 1921. The university's president, Rev. William H. Robison, made this momentous broadcast by reading the weather forecast.

After the Commerce Department began regulating this new medium, the department issued a license to the university on March 22, 1922, and randomly assigned the university station the call letters WEW.[5] Brother Rueppel interpreted WEW to stand for "We Enlighten the World." The station broadcast from

*Brother George Rueppel, an immigrant from Germany who became a Jesuit brother, could rightfully be called "The Father of St. Louis Radio." (Photo courtesy of Pius XII Memorial Library of Saint Louis University.)*

studios on the top floor of the Law School. Rueppel placed his own phonograph in front of a microphone to play music on the station. Early on, he served as the station's manager, engineer, talent scout, and announcer, and even as "Aunt Sammy," the station's local cooking authority.

During the 1930s, WEW aired "The Inter-racial Hour," presented by the Federation of Colored Catholics of the United States. The university's director of physical education, Doctor Walter Eberhardt, became the "Dean of Radio Exercisers" on WEW (and later on KMOX). The station also focused on classical music.

With competition from the new medium of television growing, the university sold the station in 1954.

*During World War I, all civilian stations were ordered to halt operations. Saint Louis University trained over 300 radio operators for the United States Army during the war.*

# Oldest Skyscraper
## The Wainwright Building
709 Chestnut St.

S t. Louis's oldest skyscraper, the Wainwright Building, is a revolutionary masterpiece of American architecture. Architect Louis Sullivan's simple but innovative approach to designing the Wainwright Building would inspire architects for years to come.

The development of steel frame construction coupled with the invention of elevators had enabled American builders to create taller and taller buildings. The architects and builders, however, were just adding floors with repetitive designs. It was Chicago architect Sullivan who saw the potential of designing

*The projecting brick piers between the second and 10th floors of the Wainwright Building create the illusion of fluting on columns. (Photo courtesy of NiNi Harris.)*

tall buildings. He believed that a skyscraper "must be every inch a proud and soaring thing, rising in sheer exultation that from bottom to top it is a unit without a single dissenting line."[6] That concept guided Sullivan's design for the Wainwright Building.

When completed in 1892, the 10-story skyscraper towered over much of Downtown St. Louis. Its magic came from Sullivan's combination of lavish ornament and vertical lines that pointed to the sky and celebrated the structure's height.

Sullivan compared his skyscraper to a column consisting of a base, a shaft, and a capital. The first two floors of the high-rise, built of massive limestone, form the sturdy base of the column. The next seven floors, with brick piers creating the illusion of fluting, form the shaft. The terra-cotta cornice, with its lush leaf scroll ornament, crowned the skyscraper like a capital crowns a column. The red coloring of the brick, the sandstone, and the terra-cotta further unified the building's design.

The new building offered 250 offices with abundant light and fresh air provided by a light court. The Wainwright Building became a prestigious address for architectural firms.

In 1974, the State of Missouri purchased the landmark Wainwright Building and transformed it into a State Office Building.

---

*Only a block north of the Wainwright Building, another of Louis Sullivan's skyscrapers opened in 1893. The Union Trust Building, at 705 Olive, was renovated and reopened in 2018 as The Hotel St. Louis.*

---

# OLDEST THEATRE ORGAN
## FOX THEATRE
**527 North Grand Blvd.**

The stage is dark, and the audience is silent in the Fox Theatre. Suddenly, the floor in front of the stage opens, and a platform rises. On the platform sits the beautiful Wurlitzer theatre pipe organ that has been there since the Fox first opened in 1929. The fingers and the feet of the organist seem to fly across the keys and the pedals as the theatre is filled with melodious sound. The Saint Louis Fox Theatre's organ is one of five identical instruments built specifically for five Fox theatres in the United States in the late 1920s. The St. Louis theatre organ is one of only two of these Wurlitzer organs that survive in their original homes; the other is in the restored Fox Theatre in Detroit.

When the St. Louis Fox Theatre opened in 1929, it wowed moviegoers with its exotic "Siamese-Byzantine" décor and its monumental scale. With more than 5,000 seats, it was one of the largest theatres in the United States. The Fox remained one of St. Louis's leading movie theatres until it closed in 1978. But thanks to the vision of Leon Strauss and his group of investors, the "Fox Associates" purchased the building in 1980 and embarked on a multimillion-dollar restoration directed by Mary Strauss, Leon's wife. The restored Fox Theatre, with the rebuilt mighty Wurlitzer organ, reopened in 1982 as a performing arts center.

The original cost of the Fox's theatre organ was $75,000. The platform on which the organ console rests can move 10 feet above

*Miss Betty Gould played the Mighty Wurlitzer for opening night at the Fox. (Photo courtesy of the Missouri Historical Society.)*

and below the floor. The organ has more than 2,500 pipes and 500 tuned percussions. In addition to the organ console, the remainder of the instrument is spread out in seven rooms on the third and fourth floors of the Fox Theatre. The sounds of an entire orchestra can be reproduced by just one person playing the Wurlitzer.

More than 80 years after it was first played, the beautiful Wurlitzer organ can still be heard on Saturday morning tours of The Fabulous Fox.

*The longtime organist at the Fox, Stan Kann, spent 22 years in Los Angeles, where he became a popular talk show guest. He made 77 appearances on Johnny Carson's Tonight Show, often demonstrating antique vacuums from his collection of odd and curious vacuum cleaners.*

# OLDEST UNIVERSITY
## SAINT LOUIS UNIVERSITY
1 North Grand Ave.

An advertisement announcing the opening of "an academy for young gentlemen" appeared in the October 23, 1818, edition of the *Missouri Gazette*. The notice stated that the academy would be conducted by four priests under the supervision of the bishop. The house of "Mrs. Alverez," a one-story residence near the site of the Old Cathedral, would host the academy. The tuition would be $12.00 per quarter.

This advertisement heralded the beginnings of Saint Louis University, which now boasts more than 127,000 alumni living in 50 states and 154 countries.

Originally, the university was more like a high school, offering the study of the Greek, Latin, French, English, Spanish, and Italian languages, along with mathematics and drawing. Though the school stumbled during its early years, by 1821 there were 65 students enrolled.

Though it only had about 5,000 residents, the city of St. Louis was becoming the staging area for explorations, military expeditions, missionary outreach, and trade routes to the American West. The early students reflected the colorful character of St. Louis. Their ranks included: Meriwether Lewis Clark, who was the son of explorer William Clark and named for his father's partner Meriwether Lewis; William Bent, who would build Bent's Fort on the Santa Fe Trail; Ninian W. Edwards,

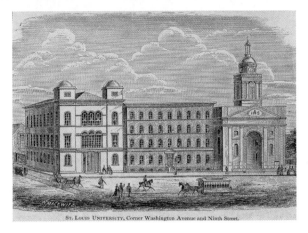

*Saint Louis University's downtown campus and the original "College Church" faced 9th Street at Washington Avenue. This line drawing of the church published in 1879 shows the cast-iron lantern that topped its octagon-shaped, brick belfry. (Illustration courtesy of NiNi Harris.)*

ST. LOUIS UNIVERSITY, Corner Washington Avenue and Ninth Street.

who became Illinois's attorney general and married a sister of Mary Todd Lincoln; Touissant Charbonneau, son of Sacajawea and the French American interpreter on the Lewis & Clark Expedition; and Louis Primeau, who became a fur trader along the Yellowstone.

Jesuit priests from Belgium who had started a seminary in Florissant took over operations of the academy in 1828. They constructed a new campus on 9th Street at Washington Avenue. Only four years later, the school received the first university charter west of the Mississippi. While St. Louis was growing exponentially as the Gateway to the West, the young Saint Louis University became a civilizing influence on the frontier. At the university on 9th Street, the classics, theology, and philosophy were taught to the future civic leaders of St. Louis and to the young men who would become the business and government leaders in the Western Territories.

*In 1889, Saint Louis University moved from downtown to its current home at Grand and Lindell Boulevards. This Midtown campus, with buildings ranging in style from Gothic Revival to mid-century modern, covers 282 acres.*

# NORTH

# —————————1817

# OLDEST AFRICAN AMERICAN CONGREGATION
## FIRST BAPTIST CHURCH OF ST. LOUIS
**3100 Bell Ave.**

A church built of rough-cut white stones in a medley of architectural styles faces Bell Avenue and the open fields of Chambers Park in North St. Louis. This church, with pointed Gothic arches and a Mission-style roof line, was once known as the First African Baptist Church. All of the city's historic African American Baptist churches grew from it. The stone church building on Bell is the third home of this congregation, which began on the riverfront and took shape with the inspiring leadership of John Berry Meachum.

First Baptist Church traces its origins to the 1817 arrival in St. Louis of two Baptist missionaries, the Reverends John Mason Peck and James Welch. They began with a Baptist Sunday school, which only 13 years earlier would have been illegal since only Catholicism was accepted under the Spanish colonial government. John Berry Meachum assisted the missionaries with the school and services. Meachum, who had been born into slavery, not only bought his own freedom and the freedom of his family, but then helped others win their freedom. In 1822, African American worshippers led by Meachum, then a layman, formed a separate branch of the church. After Meachum was ordained a minister in 1825, he and his followers officially founded the First African Baptist Church. With Meachum as its pastor, the congregation constructed a brick church building near the riverfront. At that time, the congregation's membership numbered about 220, of whom 200 were in bondage.

After the church was built, Meachum and Peck

*Though John Berry Meachum's last name was misspelled in the St. Louis City Directory published in 1840, it is remarkable that this man who was born into slavery had purchased his own freedom and was then listed. (Illustration courtesy of Carondelet Historical Society.)*

opened a Sunday school for the new congregation. There African Americans were secretly taught to read and write even when Missouri outlawed the teaching of African Americans. Known as the "Candle and Tallow School," it charged a monthly tuition of one dollar to those who could afford to pay. No one, including slaves, was ever turned away.[7] The church membership grew to over 500.

The Church moved to 14th and Clark Streets, near the present-day Enterprise Center, in 1848. The congregation grew at this location near African American settlements. After that area was industrialized, the congregation bought the former St. Mark's English Lutheran Church on Bell Avenue in 1917. The Gothic-style stone church with steeply pitched, gable roofs dated to 1880.[8]

The congregation was thriving and serving its community when a fire swept through the church on the morning of January 18, 1940. Though frostbitten firemen fought the blaze in subzero weather, only the stone shell of the church survived the fire.

In a mere 13 months, the congregation rebuilt their church, saving the stone shell and rebuilding from within. Upon entering through its Gothic doorway, visitors see two stone tablets embedded in the vestibule wall. The tablets were salvaged from the fire. Carved into one are the 10 Commandments, and the "Our Father" is written into the stone of the second.

---

*John Berry Meachum shared his personal story of how he freed himself, then his family, and then 20 slaves in these excerpts from* An Address to All the Colored Citizens of the United States, *published in 1846.*

*Meachum was born a slave in 1789. He proposed to his owner,* "to hire my time, and he granted it. By working in a saltpetre cave I earned enough to purchase my freedom . . .

"I married a slave in Kentucky, whose master soon took her to St. Louis, in Missouri. I followed her, arriving there in 1815, with three dollars in my pocket. Being a carpenter and cooper I soon obtained business, and purchased my wife and children. Since that period, I have purchased about twenty slaves, most of whom paid back the greatest part of the money, and some paid all . . .

"I commenced preaching in 1821, and was ordained as a minister of the gospel in 1825."

---

# OLDEST ICE CREAM PARLOR & CANDY SHOP
## CROWN CANDY KITCHEN
**1401 St. Louis Ave.**

At one time, there were hundreds of soda fountains, candy stores, and ice cream parlors in St. Louis. They filled corner storefronts in every neighborhood. People lined up to sit on a stool at the counter to relish a creamy, St. Louis-style malt—or if they were with friends, sit at a cozy booth where they enjoyed a sundae topped with whipped cream and pecans. The candy stores enticed St. Louisans with sweet delicacies like chocolate molasses puffs or coconut clusters.

One by one, the treasured confectionaries, fountains, and ice cream parlors disappeared from their neighborhoods. But Crown Candy continued unchanged in its Old North St. Louis neighborhood, and each year it became more of a rarity.

Crown Candy is on the first floor of a handmade brick storefront with apartments upstairs. It was built by 1883, though the cast-iron corner store entrance was completed in the early 1890s. The doorway to this over 130-year-old building acts as a portal into St. Louis's past.

The wood booths, with Formica-topped tables, are painted a cream color. The angular patterns stamped into the tin ceiling form art deco designs. The floor is a linoleum checkerboard. Old Coca-Cola trays and posters line the plate shelf above the booths.

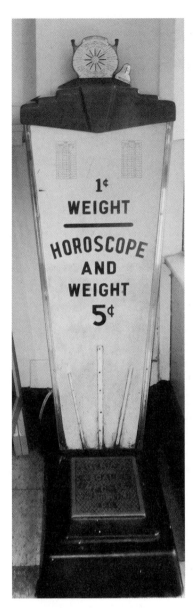

*For a penny, the old scale in the corner still offers to tell customers their weight after they have indulged on a huge sundae. (Photo by NiNi Harris.)*

Glass jars filled with colorful licorice snaps and jelly beans sit atop glass and dark wood counters filled with delicate sweets, from almond toffee to milk chocolate cherries. Even the huge, framed menu on the wall—with the offerings hand-printed with an almost Gothic font—is a relic from the past.

This unique establishment is the creation of three generations of the Greek American Karandzieff family.[9] In 1905, Harry Karandzieff immigrated to the United States in his early 20s. The candy business was a popular profession among Greek immigrants. Only eight years after coming to the United States, Harry and his friend and cousin Pete Jugaloff started Crown Candy in the old storefront at the busy corner of St. Louis Avenue and North 14th Street. According to the 1920 census, Harry, Pete, and three other family members were living above the candy store where they all worked. In 1925, they expanded their offerings by making their own ice cream.

George Karandzieff was only 10 years old when he started helping out his father Harry in the shop. Over the decades, he and his wife collected over 500 molds for making chocolate works of art, including chocolate owls (a Halloween favorite) and chocolate Thanksgiving turkeys. They used antique molds, some as old as the shop itself, to create chocolate Easter bunnies and Santas. George re-tinned some old molds, including molds crafted in Europe. All these chocolate delicacies, plus homemade ice creams with homemade syrups, combined with a sandwich menu, turned Crown Candy Kitchen into a destination.

In the 21st century, the lunch crowd favors the BLTs, which are stacked with what seems like a pound of bacon, in summer; in winter, the favorite is a bowl of chili. They finish it off with an ice cream soda, or maybe a massive sundae. On their way out the door, they pick up chocolate treats to bring back to work.

Surrounded by furnishings, treasures, and flavors that date from 1913 to the 1950s, Andy Karandzieff, the third generation of the Karandzieff family to run Crown Candy, states, "We don't do a lot of change. What you're seeing is the future—you're looking at it."[10]

---

*When Harry Karandzieff opened Crown Candy in 1913, it was at the north end of the booming North 14th Street commercial district. Competition from new suburban malls sent the area into a downward spiral. The Karandzieffs stayed and watch as their neighborhood goes through a 21st-century revival.*

---

# OLDEST CHURCH GRAVEYARD

## COLD WATER CREEK CEMETERY

15290 Old Halls Ferry Road

The roadway to the secluded 1.5-acre Cold Water Creek graveyard passes through rolling pastures on the outskirts of Florissant. A thick patch of forest surrounds the hilltop cemetery. The site of this early church graveyard remains as it was described in 1855: "obscure" and "out of sight from all public roads."[11] This "obscure" church graveyard, which started as a family plot, has outlived its church by 150 years.

The graveyard site was on the extensive Patterson family acreage in North County. The Patterson family received the lands as Spanish land grants when they arrived here in 1797 from the Carolinas. They were part of a small migration of Americans to the French settlements around St. Louis that were ruled by the Spanish colonial government. About 50 of these American families were Protestant. Officially, the Spanish commanders considered Protestantism heresy.

Assisted by the Patterson family, a Methodist minister known as "Father Clark" regularly crossed the Mississippi from Illinois to hold covert services in private homes in the Cold Water Creek area. After the Louisiana Purchase brought freedom of religion to the Louisiana Territory, the first church building was constructed on the site of the Patterson's land between 1808 and 1809. The

*Woods with a thick undergrowth surround the old church graveyard. (Photo by NiNi Harris.)*

graveyard was adjacent to the church. The first known burial at Cold Water Creek Cemetery was that of Keziah Horneday Patterson in 1809. 24 years later in the autumn of 1833, Father Clark passed away, and "his mortal remains were deposited in a burying ground, on which the church, with which he lived and died, had erected a house of worship of hewn logs."[12]

The first log church burned and was replaced by a second church built on the same site. That second church building was shared by Methodists, Baptists, and an early Presbyterian congregation until 1870. The second church is also believed to have burned. The church graveyard, however, endured.

This cemetery, which still has the feel of an early church graveyard, is the final resting place for 29 American military veterans. Three veterans of the American Revolution are buried at Cold Water Creek: John Clark, Eusebius Hubbard, and John Patterson, Sr.

*In 1963, the Daughters of the American Revolution accepted the Cold Water Creek Cemetery as a gift. As of 2020, 18 members of the DAR are at rest in Cold Water Cemetery, their "beloved treasure in the woods."*

# OLDEST COUNTRY CLUB
## GLEN ECHO COUNTRY CLUB
3401 Lucas and Hunt Road

The main entrance of Glen Echo Country Club, on Lucas and Hunt Road, is flanked by limestone piers. It opens onto a drive that meanders through the golf course to the Tudor Revival-style clubhouse. This country club, established in 1901, includes just over 144 acres and holds the oldest professional 18-hole golf course west of the Mississippi.[13]

The club's wealthy founders were mostly self-made men. They acquired the acreage for the club from the Lucas family, who had owned the land since 1817. The founders commissioned prominent course designers Jim and Robert Foulis to design a bucolic golf course. These Scottish brothers had trained at St. Andrews, the internationally famous golf club of Scotland. (Their great-grandfather had herded the grass-trimming sheep at St. Andrews.)

While transforming the acreage into 18 challenging holes, they sought to imitate and retain the natural landscape as much as possible. The names of each hole reflected something of the landscape. "Lilac

*Club members dressed in Twenties-style sporting attire. (Photo courtesy of Glen Echo Country Club.)*

*The old Hunt Mansion served as the original clubhouse for the Glen Echo Country Club. (Photo courtesy of Glen Echo Country Club.)*

Way" was named for the lilac hedge near the hole, and "Spooks" bordered the cemetery adjacent to the club.

In September 1904, the Glen Echo Country Club hosted the Olympic golf competition.[14] Seventy-seven golfers, mostly St. Louisans and Chicagoans, played in the 1904 games. Canadian George Lyon prevailed in the individual competition, and the United States Western Golf Association won the team competition.

Glen Echo's members used the old Hunt Mansion on Lucas and Hunt Road for a clubhouse until they built their current clubhouse in 1929. Designed by prominent St. Louis architect Preston Bradshaw, the new clubhouse had Old English charm.

The two-story clubhouse features stone and brick walls. Tudor-style timber and stucco fill its steeply pitched gable ends. The interior, with massive stone fireplaces, exposed beams, hardwood floors, and French doors opening to the delightful

*Glen Echo's new clubhouse, built in 1929, was characterized by Old English charm. (Photo courtesy of Glen Echo Country Club.)*

grounds, was reminiscent of the "Old World." The clubhouse cost $250,000 to build.

With its historic clubhouse and landscape, the Glen Echo Country Club was honored in 2007 with inclusion on the National Register of Historic Places.

---

*In 1892, fifteen men formed the city's first "formal golf club," the St. Louis Country Club, located on a farm near Bridgeton. In 1895, they moved to a site in Clayton, with a nine-hole course, and then moved to their current site in Ladue in 1914.*

---

# Oldest Drive-In Curb-Service Restaurant
## Chuck-A-Burger Restaurant
9025 St. Charles Rock Road

A burger with fries and a soda cost 65 cents when the Chuck-A-Burger restaurant opened in the suburb of St. John in 1957. The drive-in restaurant with curb-service looked then as it does now, more than six decades later—shiny red and white stripes, a shed roof, and a yellow ribbon of neon wrapping around the roofline and spelling out the restaurant's name: "Chuck-A-Burger."

Big cars with fin tails, bobby socks with saddle shoes, and poodle skirts were the rage when Chuck-A-Burger opened on St. Charles Rock Road, across the street from Ritenour High School. Through the years, many high school students got part-time jobs as carhops at the drive-in. Many more students went "cruising" on Friday nights and pulled into Chuck-A-Burger for dine-in or curb service.

Eventually there were eight Chuck-A-Burger restaurants around the fringes of the county. White Castles, Steak 'n Shakes, and independent restaurant diners on suburban roads also offered curb service during this heyday of car culture.

This nostalgic piece of the fifties thrives as a time warp thanks to the Stille family of North County. A native of Pagedale who served in the South Pacific during World War II, Ralph Stille was the restaurant's first manager. In 1978, he bought the St.

Charles Rock Road business from the creator of the Chuck-A-Burger chain, Bud Taylor. Stille continued with the original menu while building on its already nostalgic *Happy Days* appeal. Decades later, his son Ron Stille bought the drive-in and made additions to the menu. Ron, however, maintained the character and original dishes that now make Chuck-A-Burger a unique experience.

"We're the only drive-in, curb-service restaurant. It's not a gimmick—it's real curb service," Ron states.[15] The carhops still go to the driver's window with a pen and pad in hand to take the orders. Along with the chili (made with the original recipe), burgers, fries, and rings, Ron states, "We make our own cherry Coke." (Their recipe for the cherry syrup is a secret.) The most popular item on the menu is the double cheeseburger, known as the Super Chuck.

The menu and the original building, combined with real curb service, have

*Though there is inside service with the original counter and stools, many of the parking spots at Chuck-A-Burger are reserved for curb service.*

made Chuck-A-Burger a nostalgic destination for fans of vintage cars. "Old-school muscle cars and hot rods. Not European cars— American cars," Ron emphasizes.[16] As he spoke, a '68 Camaro, a '66 Impala, and a '70 Chevy Chevelle pulled into the lot.

---

*The carhops wear Chuck-A-Burger T-shirts, one of the few adaptations to contemporary trends. Originally the carhops, mostly girls, wore black slacks, a white shirt, a red cummerbund, and a bow tie.*

---

# Oldest Fish Market

## Kram Fish Company

1307 Biddle St.

Catfish, cod, buffalo fish, and tilapia are piled high on beds of ice in metal and glass cases in Kram Fish Company, the last vestige of a crowded, old-world ethnic neighborhood. In its heyday, the neighborhood's stores were kosher and its signs were in Hebrew. The building that houses Kram's Fish Company, Stolle's Hall, stood three stories tall. While the neighborhood disappeared, Stolle's Hall was disguised—cut down to one story and wrapped in corrugated metal. At the corners, however, the original cast-iron columns are exposed, revealing the building's 19th-century origins.

While individual shoppers are among the customers, restaurants and churches account for most of the thousands of pounds of fish sold each week at Kram's.

Proprietor Ed Kram explained that his grandfather, an immigrant from the Austrian Empire, started the business after the St. Louis World's Fair. Louis Kram had been in the feather trade, exporting feathers from Brazil to New York for the then-fashionable Gibson Girl hats. While at the fair, he met Illinois farmers who fished at Horse Shoe Lake during the winter. He and his son began peddling the fish from a horse-drawn cart. In 1908, he bought Stolle's Hall, with a popular dance hall upstairs, and opened his fish market on the first floor. Their new market was at the heart of a thriving, crowded Jewish neighborhood that

*Stolle's Hall as it looked in 1930. (Photo courtesy of Missouri Historical Society.)*

stretched west to 20th Street and overlapped with Polish, Italian, and Irish communities.

At that time there were a lot of fish markets housed in storefronts that sold fish from wooden cases, according to Kram. His grandfather expanded the market, supplying saltwater and freshwater fish. Eventually the family supplied major chains like National Food Stores. As the large chains gradually opted for fewer, larger suppliers, Kram adjusted to supply specialty markets.

---

*Louis Kram invented Jack Salmon when he could not sell the kosher fish with scales, whiting, in the St. Louis market. So he skinned it and called it Jack Salmon.*

---

# Oldest Hardware Store
## Marx Hardware
2501 North 14th St.

A bove rolls of pet fencing, a yellowed, framed portrait of James A. Garfield hangs from a shelf near the 14-foot-high ceiling. It has hung in Marx Hardware as long as anyone can remember, and probably since President Garfield died in office from an assassin's bullet in 1881. An ad for an early incarnation of a wringer washer hangs from a peg on a plaster wall, and a metal ad promoting early-20th-century wallpaper cleaner is nailed into a beadboard wall. The hardware store, with its maze of wood shelves and counters, is heated by a wood-burning iron stove.

Marx Hardware, with its generations of old ads and artifacts, is not a Disneyland re-creation of a historic hardware store. A steady stream of customers purchase trowels, toilet seats, bug killers, tools, and garden seed that are displayed in the light shed through the tall storefront windows topped by art glass transoms. A neighborhood resident buys a garden hose at the 19th-century wood counter painted battleship gray. Decades ago, the pine floors and many of the counters and shelves were painted that gray, which was sold as Navy surplus paint after World War II. Even the writing lap desk on the wood counter is painted that gray.

That lap desk, with its hinged, sloped writing top, belonged to a local post of the Grand Army of the Republic (GAR). When the number of Union veterans of the Civil War had dwindled

*Andy Marx in the doorway of Marx Hardware.
(Photo by NiNi Harris.)*

and the post disbanded, the desk was brought to the hardware store. Frederick Marx, the patriarch of the Marx family who was responsible for the family-owned hardware store, had served in the Union Army and had been a member of a GAR post.

At age 17, the German-born Marx had immigrated to St. Louis. The blond-haired, gray-eyed Marx was a blacksmith. He left his trade to serve in the Home Guard (Union loyalists) in the spring of 1861.

Following the Civil War, Marx continued in his trade, and his sons became involved in a related trade: the hardware business. In the early 1880s, Marx helped his eldest son enter into the Hoffman Hardware and Paint Company, founded in 1875. Within a few years, Henry Marx was the president of the company, and the business had moved into its current building at 2501 N. 14th St.

Ornamented cast iron framed the tall store windows of the three-story, handmade brick building. It had been used as a cigar factory and cigar store before becoming home to the hardware store.

Eventually the youngest of Marx's sons, August, managed the store. When he passed away in 1950, his son became president of the business. Then his grandson Steve Marx, the fifth generation, became president of Marx Hardware.

Six days each week, Steve Marx walks from the brick row house that his family has called home for five generations to Marx Hardware store. His brother Andy drives in from the county to help. Andy says that he enjoys the store "more now than ever before." Though so much is the same, they have changed the business continually to meet the needs of the neighborhood. Their products are smaller (no riding mowers here). They sell cleaners and convenience items along with old hardware, needed by homeowners renovating historic neighborhood homes.

---

*During the Civil War, Frederick Marx served as a private in the Home Guards commanded by North City brewer Colonel Charles G. Stifel. These North City patriots were returning from the Arsenal on May 11 when they were attacked by a mob on the corner of Walnut and Broadway. A number of the men lost their lives.*

---

# Oldest Brick House

## The Bissell Mansion

**4426 Randall Place**

T he red brick Bissell Mansion sits atop a ridge, behind a retaining wall along Interstate 70 in North St. Louis. During the late 1820s, Captain Lewis Bissell built the impressive home atop the hill overlooking the Mississippi River Valley. The veteran of the War of 1812 and his family moved into their new, spacious, two-story home in 1830.

Lewis Bissell, a native of Connecticut, came from a distinguished American military family. His grandfather, father, and uncles had served in the American Revolutionary War. His father, Russell Bissell, and his uncle, Daniel Bissell, had both commanded Fort Bellefontaine. (That fort guarded the confluence of the Mississippi and Missouri Rivers for more than two decades following the Louisiana Purchase.) Following his own military service in the War of 1812, Lewis Bissell became a sutler, supplying goods to the troops stationed at Fort Bellefontaine. Later, with partner Colonel John O'Fallon, he supplied troops stationed in the Far West.

In 1824, Lewis Bissell purchased 677 acres in what became North City. The two-story house he built on the high ground of that property had a dignified, symmetrical design. Its elegant appearance reflected the then-popular Greek Revival and Federal architectural styles. The gracious eight-room mansion

*Thick trees and shrubbery hide the front of the Bissell Mansion today. This photo, from the Historic American Building Survey, shows the Lewis Bissell House as it appeared in 1940. (Photo courtesy of the Library of Congress.)*

served as home to Captain Lewis Bissell, his family, and descendants until 1877.

Eight decades later, the Missouri Highway Department threatened to demolish the city landmark to build Interstate 70. This threat to erase the 130-year-old home rallied the incipient historic preservation movement. The mansion was saved when historic preservationist and engineer Frank Hilliker proved to the Highway Department that it was cheaper to build a retaining wall than tear down the hill with the house on top.

In recent decades, the mansion has had a new role, providing a delightful setting for popular murder mystery dinner theatre productions.

*Belgian Baron Emanuel de Hodiamont built the stone and frame Dehodiamont House, at 1951 Maple Place in North St. Louis, at about the same time that Captain Lewis Bissell built his brick mansion overlooking the river.*

# Oldest House in St. Louis County

## Casa Alvarez

**289 Rue St. Denis at St. Pierre**
**Florissant**

The home called "Casa Alvarez" in Florissant is arguably the oldest house in St. Louis County. It was built for an official with the Spanish colonial government when Florissant, then known as St. Ferdinand, was a village made up of Spanish and French Catholic settlers.

The home was built for Eugenio Alvarez, who came to St. Ferdinand around 1770 as a soldier under the command of Pedro Piernas, the Spanish lieutenant governor of Upper Louisiana. Alvarez eventually served as the military storekeeper for the Spanish government, and he became acquainted with both Pierre Laclede and Auguste Chouteau, the founders of St. Louis. In 1782, Alvarez married a young Creole woman, Josepha Crepeau, and they had three children. Their descendants maintained the home until 1905. The construction of the home, with the long ownership by the original family, documents its antiquity.

The original frame home was a single room with a large fireplace. Its log walls were constructed in French style, known as "poteaux-sur-sole." (In this method of construction, the walls were constructed of vertical logs that were mortised into a sill on

*Casa Alvarez as it appeared in the 1930s. This photo was taken as part of the Historic American Buildings Survey. (Photo courtesy of the Library of Congress.)*

a stone foundation.) A comparatively sophisticated house for the era, it had a stone basement.

By 1840, the Alvarez family had already added a staircase and a second floor, with a dormer and gable windows. Three more rooms were added in 1840. Over the years, the house was expanded to 11 rooms. Remarkably, the French character of Casa Alvarez is immediately apparent despite the additions.

In 1976, Casa Alvarez was named to the National Register of Historic Places.

*In 1818, the first classes of St. Louis College (later Saint Louis University) were conducted in a home on the St. Louis riverfront belonging to Eugenio Alvarez's widow, Josepha Crepeau Alvarez.*

# OLDEST PUBLIC HOUSING
## THE NEIGHBORHOOD GARDENS APARTMENT COMPLEX
7th, 8th, Biddle, and O'Fallon Sts.

At first glance, the old Neighborhood Gardens apartment complex appears almost severe. One contemporary source described the walls of the Neighborhood Gardens's three-story buildings "as plain as a modernistic drawing."[17] A closer look reveals the patterns in their brick walls, with designs that give the buildings a subtle beauty.

Though the courtyards of these apartments have been converted into parking lots, and dwellings have been combined to create larger apartments, Neighborhood Gardens still expresses the dramatic modern movement in architecture and a historic commitment to provide comfortable and healthy housing for working families.

Construction of the Neighborhood Gardens, covering an entire block just north of downtown, was announced in the spring of 1934. "Slums" had been cleared, and The Housing Division of the Public Works Administration (one of Roosevelt's New Deal employment programs) provided a $638,000 loan for Neighborhood Gardens. The directors of the Neighborhood Association, a local concern, furnished the $100,000 balance. The Neighborhood Association's director, J.A. Wolf, modeled the complex after successful housing projects in Germany and Vienna. It was the architect, however, who gave the big complex intimacy, comfort, and beauty.

*An aerial view showing the completed Neighborhood Gardens Housing Projects as it appeared in June of 1935. (Photo courtesy of the Missouri Historical Society.)*

P. John Hoener, of the architectural firm of Hoener, Baum, and Froese, made the complex neighborhood scale by designing 23 individual buildings. Though many of the buildings shared walls, each had its own entrance, surrounded by ornamental brickwork. Each apartment had a balcony that looked into the courtyards. Sandboxes and a wading pool created a delightful play space for children. The family-friendly apartments offered St. Louis's first baby-carriage garage, with spaces for at least 25 carriages.

The complex successfully provided pleasant housing for workers who could walk to jobs downtown. In the 1940s, before he became a great American playwright, William Inge lived in the Neighborhood Gardens.

By the 1990s, however, the complex sat abandoned and empty. A $10,000,000 renovation completed in 2005 reduced the number of apartments from 252 to 144 larger units, while restoring the exceptional brickwork in the complex.

---

*A* St. Louis Star-Times *reporter commented on the efficiency of the kitchens, stating, "Everything the housewife needs in the preparation of a meal is within easy reach, and there is a place for everything. If she has a slovenly kitchen the crime will be on her head, and not the architect's."[18]*

---

# OLDEST MUNICIPALITY IN ST. LOUIS COUNTY

## FLORISSANT

**North County**

The maps of North St. Louis County show miles of sprawling cul-de-sacs surrounding a small square filled with a grid of blocks. That square—with streets named for saints like St. Antoine, St. Denis, St. Francois, St. Catherine—is Old Town Florissant. While Florissant's cul-de-sacs reflect the post-World War II suburban building boom, the streets of Old Town reach back to Florissant's origins in the late 18th century.

A few years after Pierre Laclede founded St. Louis, French fur trappers settled in the valley about 15 miles to the northwest. The rich, dark soil led early settlers to call the area Fleurissant or Florissant, meaning flourishing or flowering.[19] Florissant's square grid of village streets probably dates to the formation of the first civil government shortly after 1786. That was when the Spanish colonial authorities appointed Francois Dunegant as the settlement's military commandant. Four years later, a census counted 40 inhabitants in the village, which was officially named St. Ferdinand in honor of the Spanish Crusader King. While nearby St. Louis was the center of a tremendous trade network, Florissant's villagers farmed their rich land.

Florissant was first incorporated as a town in 1829, and in 1857 was chartered as a city by the state of Missouri. Still, Florissant grew slowly. The 1880 census counted only 817 residents in Florissant. They were mostly descendants of the early settlers. In the early 1880s, their suburban city had six general stores, two hotels, three wagon and blacksmith shops, four shops, three tailor shops, two harness shops, one shoe manufacturer, one tin shop, and two physicians.

Over the next 70 years, Florissant grew to a population of only 3,737, and the St. Louis County municipality still had the feel of a small town. Bulldozers, however, were rumbling through the area. Suddenly it seemed like tract-house subdivisions were growing up overnight. During the 1950s, the population grew tenfold to 38,166 and was still growing.

**Visit Historic**

*Florissant*

**Missouri**

"In the Valley of
The Flowers
Near the Gateway
To the West"

☆

The Only Suburban City That Shares
Nearly All of the 200 Year History
With St. Louis

☆

This Program Sponsored by
**Florissant
Bicentennial of St. Louis
Committee**

*Florissant published a historic sites brochure as part of St. Louis's bicentennial celebration in 1964. (Brochure courtesy of Carondelet Historical Society.)*

The new residents, however, were helping to form preservation groups to save threatened historic landmarks in the booming community. When St. Louis celebrated its bicentennial in 1964, the Florissant Bicentennial of St. Louis Committee bragged that Florissant was "the only suburban City that shares nearly all of the 200 year history with St. Louis."

---

*In 1964, Florissant boasted a population of 55,000 and claimed that it was "the 7th city in population in the State of Missouri."*[20]

---

# Oldest Polish Sausage Shop
## Piekutowski's European-Style Sausage
4100 N. Florissant

A corner storefront in a forgotten North City neighborhood is the home of Piekutowski's sausage—a mecca for people who relish rich flavors from the past. Though the unique sausage is sold at a number of groceries around the area, many customers prefer to buy it where it is made. They come in numbers from St. Charles and the Metro East. One young man from New York City makes Piekutowsi's his last stop on his regular visits to St. Louis, because he can't find sausage like it in the Big Apple.

Piekutowski's offers 10 kinds of sausage, though the three traditional sausages made by the original butcher are in the most demand. Ted (Thaddeus) Piekutowski, assisted by his grandson, starts with choosing fine cuts of meat. He mixes them in specific proportions and with various combinations of eight spices for each type of sausage. Then they grind the sausage, feeding it right into the casing.

The recipes for the Krakow sausage, small Krakow, and Kielbasa, commonly called Polish sausage, originated with Leon Ziemba, who first opened the shop in 1916. Ziemba had emigrated from Poland in 1900 and became a citizen. His shop was at 10th Street and Cass Avenue, at the heart of a Polish

*Shelves of Polish jams, pickles, and horseradish in the sausage shop.
(Photo by NiNi Harris.)*

neighborhood. He hired a neighborhood teenager, Thaddeus
Zigmund Piekutowski, to help him at the shop. Thaddeus was
the son and grandson of Polish immigrants who lived in a
second-floor apartment over the butcher shop. It was young
Thaddeus Piekutowski who measured the spices and wrote down
Ziemba's recipes.

When Ziemba passed away in 1940, he left the butcher shop
to Piekutowski. Thaddeus's sons Ted and Ken carried on the
trade and the traditions after him. Today Ted is assisted by
his daughter, Connie Koch, and the fourth generation of the
Piekutowski family, Cory and Tara, who are learning the trade
and the recipes.

In 1957, when eminent domain was taking much of the old neighborhood around Cass for the interstate and housing projects, Piekutowski's moved to the brick storefront on North Florissant. Along with the butcher counter filled with fresh sausage, the shop is filled with shelves stacked with pickles, horseradish and kapusta (kraut).

---

*When the Polish Pope John Paul II visited St. Louis in 1999, he requested Piekutowski's sausage. He remembered it from 1980, when he came here as the archbishop of Krakow.*

---

# Oldest Vigil
## The Pink Sisters at Mount Grace Chapel
1438 E. Warne

Inside of a chapel that glows pink, only 100 yards from trucks roaring down Interstate 70, Roman Catholic sisters pray continually, night and day. Known as "The Pink Sisters" because their uniform is a bright pink and white habit, this order of nuns has maintained a constant vigil since their chapel in a now-battered North St. Louis neighborhood opened on June 7, 1928. When the sisters began their vigil, their neighborhood was prosperous. Blocks of handsome houses faced lush O'Fallon Park on high ground that gently sloped down to the Mississippi River and the busy industries that lined it. Since their vigil began, the surrounding neighborhood suffered through the Great Depression, and then its young men fought in World War II. A highway cut a gash through the neighborhood. While the neighborhood experienced economic decline, The Pink Sisters have maintained this place they describe as "where heaven and earth meet."

A stone and iron fence frames the enclave of these cloistered sisters. The grounds and the extraordinary Mount Grace Chapel radiate serenity. The interior of the Renaissance-inspired chapel is brilliant with shades of pink, bronze, and marble. Golden cherubs top the columns lining the nave. The design focuses attention on the marble altar, where a consecrated communion host is displayed in an ornate monstrance for veneration. While a constant stream of visitors drop in for quiet prayer, the sisters

*Everything glows pink within these chapel doors, where Catholic sisters have been praying night and day since 1928. (Photo by NiNi Harris.)*

maintain their vigil in the front of the chapel, separated from the visitors by an ornate metal grille.

Their vigil, which is called "perpetual adoration" is the mission of the Pink Sisters, a religious order founded in Holland in 1896. A Catholic philanthropist, Mrs. Theresa Backer Kulage, brought this order of nuns to St. Louis. Her German immigrant parents made a fortune as flour millers and flour merchants. Her German husband, Joseph Kulage, made his fortune in St. Louis's thriving brick industry. As a widow, Theresa Kulage funded the chapel and residence for the sisters on the site of her own home in North City.

She and the sisters clearly influenced the design of the uniquely feminine chapel. They carefully directed the design and crafting of the centerpiece of the chapel, the Carrara marble altar that was hand chiseled in Pietrasanta, Italy.

---

*The 18 sisters currently maintaining the perpetual adoration are from the Netherlands, Germany, Philippines, and Puerto Rico as well as the United States.*

---

# SOUTH

# OLDEST COOKIE BAKERY
## DAD'S COOKIE COMPANY
**3854 Louisiana Ave.**

Entering the century-old storefront in the Dutchtown neighborhood reveals marble-topped counters, glass display cases, and old, dark-stained woodwork. The floors are made of small, colorful, ceramic tiles. Even the scale on the counter, with its metal bowl, is vintage. Packages and bins of Dad's Cookies fill the shelves and cases of this shop, which hasn't changed since the Renz family started baking oatmeal cookies in 1938.

The Hastey brothers, the fourth generation of this German American family to run the bakery, order oatmeal, flour, and sugar by the half-ton to bake over six million cookies each year.

The Renz family, however, was supplying their neighborhood with baked goodies for decades before they focused on oatmeal cookies. German American baker

*Millions of cookies are sold out of this tiny Dutchtown neighborhood store. (Photo by NiNi Harris.)*

John Jay Renz built the handsome, two-story, brick storefront in 1911. Ornamental brickwork, stonework, and shaped wood brackets all highlight the facade of the dark brick building.

Renz opened his traditional South Side German bakery in the storefront, with the room-sized brick oven in the bakery kitchen. Like other shopkeepers of that day, his family lived in the second-floor apartments.

The next generation of the baking family took a step that set the Renz family business apart. Henry Renz, Sr. bought the St. Louis franchise for Dad's Original Scotch Oatmeal cookies. According to Renz's descendants, "Dad's Original Scotch Oatmeal Cookies arrived in California from Scotland around 1900." The company became one of the "country's first franchised businesses." Other franchises operated in two dozen cities across the nation. Eventually all the other franchises disappeared.

Meanwhile, Henry "Hank" Renz, Jr., and then the next generation, the Hastey Brothers, carried on their South St. Louis business using the original oatmeal cookie recipe. The flavor of the crispy, crunchy cookies—dipped in a glass of milk or in a cup of coffee, or eaten with vanilla ice cream—has created a following for the bakery that spans generations.

---

*The patriarch of this baking family emigrated from Germany in 1884 and became a naturalized citizen of the United States in 1911, the same year he built the bakery in Dutchtown.*

---

# Oldest Pretzel Factory

## Gus' Pretzels

1820 Arsenal St.

Lines often extend out the door of the South St. Louis storefront at the corner of Arsenal Street and Lemp Avenue, the home of Gus' Pretzels. The customers wind their way through the shop waiting to buy a straight pretzel with cheese or to pick up an order of 100 pretzels for a party. While waiting, they look through huge windows into the bakery and watch the staff rolling or twisting pretzels. Beginning with mixing the dough for seven minutes, allowing the dough to rise, rolling the pretzels, and then 15 minutes in the oven, each pretzel requires 40 minutes to create. The resulting tasty treats, still warm from the oven, are part of the collective sensory memory of St. Louisans.

Gus' Pretzels began in 1920, when a German American boilermaker was injured in a factory. After losing an eye in a riveting accident, Frank Ramsperger could not find work in his trade. Perhaps inspired by his widowed mother, who had

*The Koebbe family posed in Gus' Pretzels bakery. (Photo courtesy of Gus' Pretzels.)*

supported her young family as a baker, Ramsperger began baking pretzels in the basement of his South St. Louis home. By the end of World War II, he had moved his pretzel business to a former bakery building on Arsenal at Lemp.

In 1952, Ramsperger's son-in-law, August Koebbe, Sr., took over the bakery and officially named it Gus' Pretzel Shop. He and his wife Marcella worked with street vendors who sold their fresh-baked, salty treasures at intersections all over town. They baked stick pretzels, so the peddlers could entice customers with the golden-brown treats peeking from the tops of the brown paper bags.

As toddlers and babies, Gus and Marcella's seven children spent time in high chairs and playpens at the back of the bakery while their parents worked. When someone cried or was teething, it was easy for Gus Sr. and Marcella to stick a pretzel in their mouth.[21]

Gus Jr. bought the business from his dad in January 1980 and married his college sweetheart, Suzanne, that August. "She heard I was rolling in dough," said Gus Jr.[22] Gus Jr. and Suzanne expanded the pretzel business, baking cinnamon and garlic-butter pretzels as well as pretzel sandwiches with the brats baked inside the dough.

As the fourth generation, Gus Koebbe III, takes over the century-old pretzel bakery, it has become a relished part of St. Louis's culinary traditions.

---

*The bake shop uses a minimum of 5,000 pounds of flour each week. Each day the Koebbe family and employees bake more than 5,000 golden-brown pretzels.*

---

# OLDEST BALLROOM
## THE CASA LOMA
3354 Iowa at Cherokee St.

The 5,000-square-foot dance floor at the Casa Loma Ballroom regularly accommodates hundreds of couples. Sometimes they are enjoying ballads from the 1940s, and at other times it could be a Latin band or rock 'n' roll. Teenagers might be sharing the same dance floor with 80-year-olds.

This ballroom is unique today, but when the waltz and the foxtrot were popular, ballrooms were part of St. Louis social life. When brothers and commercial developers Eugene and Harry Freund opened the first ballroom on this corner of Iowa and Cherokee in 1927, girls with bobbed hair were dancing the Charleston. The Freunds called the ballroom "The Cinderella." Later operators adopted the name the "Casa Loma Ballroom." Ella Fitzgerald, a young Frank Sinatra, and Harry James and His Orchestra performed at the South City ballroom.

In 1940, the popular ballroom went up in flames. The Freunds hired architect William Wedemeyer to design the new, stylish Casa Loma. The three-story building, which cost $150,000, featured the sweeping curves of the then-popular art deco movement. Its pale brick and stylized terra-cotta gave the building a modern look. The ballroom boasted a "floating dance floor," made of maple laid on top of a one-inch-thick bed of rubber. Circular staircases led to the balcony overlooking the dance floor. On November 15, 1940, when the doors opened on the new Casa Loma, 1,100 people crowded the floor to dance to the music of Herbie Kay and His Orchestra.

With the continued popularity of dance bands, the Casa Loma hosted Guy Lombardo and His Orchestra and Latin dance music pioneer Xavier Cugat. Local stars like Bob Kuban and the In-Men filled the ballroom with teenagers. On Saturday afternoons, high schoolers jammed the dance floor.

With hippies and acid rock, however, dance bands disappeared from youth culture. Many of the old ballrooms around the nation, catering to a diminishing audience, faded and closed.

Meanwhile, the Casa Loma remained a place where you could feel the rhythms of another era. Then, in 1990, Pat and Roseann Brannon bought the by-then-historic ballroom and made the commitment to keep alive this part of American culture.

---

*While the Casa Loma filled the upper floors of the building that wrapped around the corner of Iowa at Cherokee, retail shops including Libson Hosiery, Shaw-Harbor Dry Goods, Walgreens, and a restaurant once filled the first-floor storefronts.*

---

*Fighting the fire that swept through the ballroom on January 19, 1940, left the remains of the original building encased in ice. (Photo courtesy of NiNi Harris.)*

# Oldest Billiards Table Manufacturer

## A.E. Schmidt Billiards Co.
720 Koeln St.

In a 1970s corrugated metal factory in the Carondelet neighborhood, artisans carry on a craft much like their German ancestors have for 170 years. The Schmidt family's business not only survived the Great Depression and two world wars, but it has survived an effort to break the billiard-table industry in the United States.

Kurt Schmidt, the fifth generation operating the family-owned business, explains that a few years ago, there were approximately 150 companies in the United States making 100 or more tables per year. Then subsidized Chinese companies entered the market, selling their tables for less than the cost of the slate for the tabletop. It "decimated" the industry in the United States.[23] Only six American manufacturers, including A.E. Schmidt Billiards Co., survived. This St. Louis firm is the oldest company manufacturing billiards tables in this country.

Kurt Schmidt credits the company's survival to their custom work. A.E. Schmidt offers 70 styles of tables that range from Victorian to contemporary styles. While most customers choose maple, oak, or poplar, Schmidt offers a choice of 10 woods and creates personalized, inlaid designs using other woods, metal, or

**A. E. SCHMIDT CO.   1809-11 Olive St.   ST. LOUIS, MO.**
**THE LINCOLN**
CAN BE HAD WITH OR WITHOUT STREAMLINE EQUIPMENT
*MADE OF SOLID OAK (Not Veneered)*

*An old advertisement for the solid oak, Lincoln model pool table crafted by A. E. Schmidt Co. at the turn of the century. (Advertisement courtesy of A.E. Schmidt Company.)*

shell. The skill and craftsmanship required for this work can be traced back through generations of the family-owned business.

Ernst Schmidt, the patriarch of the family and a master craftsman, was among the wave of German immigrants settling in St. Louis in the late 1840s. He set up shop with a shingle that read: "Ernst Schmidt Ivory Turner and Dealer in Ivory Billiard Balls, Ten Pin Balls and Smoking Pipes."[24] He learned English, but most of his instructions were written on a chalkboard in German. He brought his son Oscar into the trade at age five. Oscar expanded the business into the manufacturing and repairing of pool tables. Each generation has adapted the company to address new challenges. Five members of the sixth generation of the Schmidt family are among the 17 employees at A.E. Schmidt Billiards Company. Each year they produce 500 mostly customized billiard tables.

*Even when St. Louis was a rugged fur trading outpost, the settlers played billiards. A deed dated April 2, 1767, documents that Jean Comparios sold "a house now used as a billiard room" for 550 livres that could be paid in fur pelts.[25]*

# Oldest Bohemian Landmark
## The Front Wall of St. John Nepomuk Chapel
1625 S. 11th St.

The facade of the Gothic-style St. John Nepomuk Chapel is the oldest landmark of this ethnic community that is still part of the Bohemian American experience in St. Louis.

There was a time in St. Louis when Bohemian Americans shopped at Bohemian bakeries, sang in Bohemian choirs, joined Bohemian gymnasiums, published a Bohemian-language newspaper, and saved their money at Bohemian Savings and Loan. The St. Louis Public Library estimated in 1921 that there were 12,000 to 15,000 Bohemian Americans in the city, mostly living in the tightly knit "Bohemian Hill" neighborhood. The epicenter of this crowded and vibrant community was at 11th Street and Lafayette Avenue, the site of St. John Nepomuk Bohemian Catholic Parish and near the old Bohemian National Hall.

The community had begun with Bohemians settling in the Soulard neighborhood in 1848. Soon their numbers had grown enough to form a Roman Catholic parish, St. John Nepomuk. Parishioners built a temporary frame church and school. The growing parish replaced their frame church with an impressive brick-and-stone Gothic-style church atop the hill at 11th Street and Lafayette in 1870.

On the afternoon of May 27, 1896, a devastating tornado ripped through South Saint Louis, tearing apart Bohemian Hill. All the parish buildings, which then included two schools and a parish hall, were badly damaged, but none worse than their beautiful Gothic church. The tornado toppled its steeple, peeled off the roof, then battered down the brick walls of St. John Nepomuk Church. Only the front wall still stood—with the year 1870 carved into the keystone over the main door.

The Bohemian parishioners rebuilt the church in 1896, around the original front wall and doorways from 1870.

The Bohemians restored their crowded, ethnic neighborhood, and it continued to thrive through World War II. Following the

CHURCH OF ST. JOHN OF NEPOMUK, SOULARD AND ELEVENTH STREETS

*Only the front wall of St. John Nepomuk Church survived the tornado of 1896. (Illustration courtesy of NiNi Harris.)*

war, 50 blocks of Bohemian Hill were taken by eminent domain for the construction of Interstate 55, Interstate 44, and a housing project. The houses, corner shops, and even the Bohemian National Hall were razed, and the people were scattered. Though most of its neighborhood was erased, the church remained.

Despite being forced to move, Bohemian Americans continued to support their church. They still attend Sunday Mass at the 124-year-old church, with a front wall that is 150 years old.

---

*The St. John Nepomuk Parish school buildings were converted into condominiums. Supporters still hold fundraisers for the parish church, which was demoted to a chapel, in the parish hall that dates to 1892.*

---

# OLDEST CEMETERY
## JEFFERSON BARRACKS NATIONAL CEMETERY

Rows of thousands of white marble headstones cover the grassy hillsides and slopes of Jefferson Barracks National Cemetery. The simple beauty of this sacred landscape could not be more dramatic.

When Jefferson Barracks Cemetery was declared a national cemetery in 1866, it had already served as a final resting place for decades. It began as the post cemetery for Jefferson Barracks. The first known and recorded burial at the cemetery was for Eliza Ann Lash. The 18-month-old baby girl of a garrison officer died on August 5, 1827.

The frontier military post of Jefferson Barracks had been established a year earlier. It was the westernmost post at that time, and had grown into the largest post in the United States by the 1840s.

The original post graveyard is in the northeast part of the current cemetery, not far from the old parade grounds. It sits atop high ground overlooking the Mississippi, with the Illinois bluffs in the distance.

During the early years, a crude wooden fence kept wild animals out of the small cemetery, which was maintained by soldiers.

The burials in that section chronicled early life at the post. It is the final resting place of Second Lieutenant Charles O. May, who died on January 19, 1830, from wounds suffered in a duel that took place at the north gate of the Barracks. Captain Pewben

*The rows of thousands of marble headstones awe visitors to Jefferson Barracks Cemetery into silence.*

Holmes was buried there after he perished in the line of duty on April 29, 1857. He was a member of the "2nd Dragoons." This new branch of the military, later renamed the Cavalry, was organized at Jefferson Barracks. By the time of the Civil War, 600 soldiers and civilians were buried at the post cemetery. Soon the post cemetery served as the resting place for Civil War soldiers who died in the hospital at Jefferson Barracks.

As the death toll rose during the Civil War, the United States government struggled to respectfully bury fallen Union troops.

This need led to an 1862 bill authorizing the purchase of land to be used as "a national cemetery for the soldiers who shall die in the service of the country." Jefferson Barracks Cemetery was officially named one of the first national cemeteries in 1866.

The old post cemetery grew by thousands of graves as Union dead were recovered from temporary burial sites at other Missouri locations including Cape Girardeau, Pilot Knob, Warsaw, and Rolla. Their remains, along with those buried at the old Arsenal Island, the Wesleyan Cemetery at Grand and Laclede Avenues in Midtown, and at sites across Arkansas were reinterred at Jefferson Barracks. Whenever possible, the Union dead were interred in sections by state. The 10,200 Union dead included 1,067 African Americans.

In the 1870s, the original wood markers were replaced with the simple, poignant white marble headstones that seem to glisten in the sunlight. At the same time, all honorably discharged men, and later their families, became eligible for burial at the national cemeteries.

---

*Among the more than 560 group burials are 123 victims of a 1944 Japanese massacre of POWs in the Philippines. The brutalized POWs were burned alive before they could be liberated.*

---

The cemetery kept expanding, its acres filled with the graves of veterans of all American wars, including Revolutionary War veteran Private Richard Gentry, whose headstone reads "Present at the Capture of Cornwallis at Yorktown," and First Lieutenant

Michael Joseph Blassie of the US Air Force, who was shot down in Vietnam in 1972.[26]

Jefferson Barracks Cemetery, one of the oldest of 150 national cemeteries, is the final resting place of more than 226,200 veterans and their family members. The cemetery covers 331 acres, and the National Cemetery Association is trying to acquire more acres. Officials with the National Cemetery Administration stated that Jefferson Barracks Cemetery and the other national cemeteries of the United States "offer testimony to the desire of a grateful nation to appropriately commemorate the Americans who have served their nation in the armed forces."[27]

---

*Also buried in Jefferson Barracks Cemetery are 1,126 Confederates, many of whom were prisoners who died at the post. While the tops of the Americans' headstones form a gentle arch, the tops of the Confederate headstones are peaked.*

---

# 1880

# OLDEST AFRICAN AMERICAN CHURCH BUILDING
## QUINN A.M.E. CHAPEL
225 Bowen St.

This historic church building was originally constructed as a farmers market in 1869 by what was then the city of Carondelet. The handsome market faced a street leading up the hill from the Mississippi near the site where Carondelet was founded in 1767. Built of handmade brick, the market measured 51 feet long and 42 feet wide. It had a gabled roof and large, arched windows resting on stone sills.

Shortly after the market was completed, the City of St. Louis annexed Carondelet, which then became a city neighborhood. After the annexation, the market appears to have stood vacant for years.

In 1880, an African Methodist Episcopal (A.M.E.) congregation bought the market building to convert into its church, Quinn Chapel. The roots of this congregation date to about 1845 when the A.M.E.[28] evangelist Winston Early formed a class for prayer meetings in Carondelet. These meetings, held on a farm or a plantation near Broadway and Eiler Street, were conducted while slavery was still legal and practiced in Missouri. The meetings

*This photo shows Quinn Chapel as it appeared in 1945. The church bell was manufactured by the Fulton Casting Works in Pittsburgh and dated 1847. (Photo courtesy of Carondelet Historical Society.)*

spawned two African American congregations: the Freedman's Church and Quinn Chapel A.M.E. Church.[29]

Members of the A.M.E. congregation bought the old Market building, only five blocks south of the site of the prayer meetings, for $600, payable at a rate of $120 a year. In 1882, they dedicated their church Quinn Chapel in honor of William Paul Quinn, an A.M.E. missionary and later the first African American Methodist bishop.[30] On December 28, 1885, the congregation paid off its loan and owned its church, free of debt. The members added a square belfry and a new entrance to the front of the church at the turn of the century.[31] The square belfry rises eight feet above the peak of the gable and is topped by a wood cornice.

The bell in the new belfry was rescued from a burned boat on the Mississippi River.

With historical information provided by longtime members, Quinn Chapel was listed on the National Register of Historic Places in 1974, making it one of the first St. Louis sites to achieve that designation.

---

*In 1869, the Freedman's church (later known as St. John's African Methodist Church) was built at Eiler and Broadway near the site of the original prayer meetings. It burned but was rebuilt, and the congregation remained active into at least the late 1880s.*

---

# Oldest Convent
## The Motherhouse of the Sisters of St. Joseph of Carondelet
**6400 Minnesota**

A crenellated stone wall frames the massive, red brick Motherhouse of the Sisters of St. Joseph in the Carondelet neighborhood. The Motherhouse, which sits atop a hill and overlooks the Mississippi, was completed in 1899, when its Romanesque-style chapel was built. The original wing, however, dates to 1840.

That 180-year-old convent building, an elegant, Greek Revival-style structure, was a gift to the sisters from a wealthy and prominent Irish St. Louisan, Mrs. Ann Mullanphy. From 1836, when the sisters arrived in Carondelet from France, until the completion of the brick convent, the sisters had lived in a primitive log cabin.

The log cabin had two rooms and a hall. The first three sisters and the four orphans they took in lived in the cabin. During the day, they turned the cabin into Carondelet's first school, with 20 students. The students used boxes or logs for seats. With these humble beginnings, this order of nuns—founded in mid-17th-century France to work with the needy and the deaf—established themselves in the United States.

The Greek Revival brick convent, which cost $1,050 to construct, became the first of seven wings of the Motherhouse that were built during the 19th century. In this hilltop convent in

Carondelet, the sisters founded St. Joseph's Academy, St. Joseph's Institute for the Deaf, and Fontbonne College.

In 2000, the Sisters of St. Joseph of Carondelet began a complete restoration and renovation of the historic Motherhouse. Today, the Motherhouse serves as home to the St. Louis province administrative offices, various outreach ministries, and approximately 20 of the sisters.

---

*The bedrooms were in the attic of the original log cabin. To reach the bedrooms, the sisters had to climb a ladder propped against the cabin and enter through an attic window. The roof was so inadequate that the sisters occasionally had to brush snow from the bedding.*

---

*This lithograph published in 1860 shows the brick convent building that replaced the original log cabin convent of the Sisters of St. Joseph of Carondelet. (Lithograph courtesy of Carondelet Historical Society.)*

# OLDEST DRUGSTORE
## WINKELMANN SONS DRUG COMPANY
3300 Meramec St.

The name Winkelmann is written in art glass over the shop windows of the brick and cast-iron storefront at the heart of the Dutchtown neighborhood. That three-story building at the corner of Meramec Street and Virginia Avenue, where the old streetcar line turned the corner, has been home to this family-run, independent pharmacy since 1913. Daniel P. Winkelmann III is the pharmacist and president of the drugstore that was started by his great-grandfather and great-grand-uncle. The roots of this Dutchtown neighborhood drugstore, however, reach into 19th-century St. Louis.

When the streets were dirt and the sidewalks were brick, a one-story, frame, Greek Revival-style pharmacy building stood on the Dutchtown corner. "Maryville Pharmacy" was probably named after the new Maryville Academy (the forerunner of Maryville University), which was located a few blocks to the east on Meramec Street. The proprietor of the pharmacy, Adolf Blitz, also sold cigars and "soda water." In the early 1880s, Irish American physician Robert J. Reilly moved his office into the frame storefront along with Blitz's drugstore.[32]

The surrounding small German settlement started booming with the arrival of the electrified streetcar. When it began service in 1893, the streetcars brought new residents, increased business, and spurred new construction. In 1895, Jennie Reilly, Dr. Reilly's

*The art glass transom window announcing Winkelmann's drugstore was installed after the Winkelmanns bought the building in 1913. (Photo by NiNi Harris.)*

widow, had the small frame storefront moved to the back of the property. She then built the three-story brick store and apartments, costing $8,800, on the corner site. Later, the Reillys' son operated the pharmacy in the new, modern storefront.

Meanwhile in nearby Carondelet, a stern German shoemaker encouraged his sons to find a profession so they wouldn't end up working long hours in the zinc works. Those sons, Ernst A. and Henry Winkelmann, both decided to be pharmacists in an era when neighborhood pharmacies with soda fountains were becoming centerpieces of community life. After graduating from the St. Louis College of Pharmacy, Ernst in 1892 and Henry in 1896, they worked at other pharmacies before opening their own. While building his pharmaceutical business, Ernst and his wife Carla raised 12 children. Six of their boys became pharmacists who opened independent pharmacies. Two of Henry's children became pharmacists.

In 1913, Ernst and Henry opened Winkelmann Sons Drug Company at Meramec Street and Virginia Avenue.

---

*In the era before chain drugstores controlled the market, the Winkelmann name became synonymous with neighborhood pharmacies. In 1976, the* St. Louis Post-Dispatch *reported that 23 members of this family had been or were pharmacists in the St. Louis area.*[33]

---

# —1877

# Oldest Florist
## Walter Knoll Florist
2765 LaSalle St.

In a huge studio on LaSalle Street, a dozen floral designers with Walter Knoll Florist work at long counters creating centerpieces for a wedding reception. They are sculptors with floral displays, placing hydrangea blooms from South America among greenery from Florida. Hoses hang from the ceiling over each workstation, each one releasing flower food that lengthens the life of the colorful blooms. These floral designers are carrying on a tradition; the bouquets, centerpieces, corsages, and floral arrangements created by Walter Knoll Florist have been part of St. Louis family celebrations, holidays, funerals, proms, and weddings for over 140 years.

Walter Knoll's 100 employees (16 of whom are family members) operate three neighborhood stores and a landscaping division, in addition to their large studio, store, greenhouse offering garden plants for sale, and wholesale flower business on LaSalle Street. The family-owned company also is part of a flower co-op in Quito, Equador, where long-stemmed roses are groomed for floral arrangements.

The earliest record of this family business is a listing in the 1877 St. Louis City Directory for John A. Knoll, "florist," under the heading "Florists and Nurserymen." At that time, the Bavarian immigrant was in his early fifties. He and his wife were raising their family on land adjacent to Carondelet Park. (Census records indicate that the family had been gardening that land since at least 1870.) His son John George continued on the family homestead and grew the business along with the roses. In fact, the Knolls were the first commercial rose growers west of the Mississippi, and they were allowed to grow the patented American Beauty Rose. The Knoll family cultivated their roses year-round in greenhouses. By the late 1890s, their home, floral shop, and long greenhouses extended the length of a city block. The greenhouses were heated by a row of holes in the middle of the floor that were filled with burning coals.

Sophie, the widow of John George, divided his florist business among his three sons, creating names synonymous with the floral industry in St. Louis: John Knoll Florist, Herman Knoll Florist, and Walter Knoll Florist.

Eventually, Walter Knoll Florist was buying flowers from a 300- to 500-mile radius. The next generation, brothers Chuck, David, and Walter, decided to expand their business into a regional company. In 1990, they bought out the other descendant Knoll florists. Though the original homestead and greenhouses across from Carondelet Park had been taken by the Missouri Highway Department during the construction of Interstate-55, the brothers found another historic site for the expanding floral business.

In 2003, the Knoll family moved their headquarters from their shop on Chippewa to 2.5 acres with shop buildings, studios, coolers, warehouses, and greenhouses on historic Florists' Row on LaSalle Street. While reinvigorating Florists' Row, which had been the produce row of the floral industry, Walter Knoll Florist doubled their operations. In addition to selling bedding plants and tomato plants for the garden and expanding their landscaping division, artists at Walter Knoll Florist create floral arrangements with roses from Ecuador, sprays of orchids from Thailand, tulips from Holland, and calla lilies from New Zealand.

---

*Florist Row, a sort of Main Street for wholesale florists, sprung up on the 2700 block of LaSalle Street in 1927. An association of floral companies constructed the storefronts on LaSalle Street to accommodate florists then being uprooted from western downtown by the building of Soldiers Memorial. Florist Row has expanded to include two-and-one-half blocks of LaSalle Street extending west of Jefferson.*

---

# Oldest Collection of Flowering Plants
## The Orchid Collection
**Missouri Botanical Garden**

The annual orchid show held at the Missouri Botanical Garden, featuring brilliantly colored tropical blooms displayed amongst lush foliage, is a treasured escape from the sight of mid-winter's bare branches set against gray skies. Orchids are one of the largest families of flowering plants (with about 27,800 known orchid species), and the Missouri Botanical Garden's orchid collection is one of the largest and finest in the United States.

The orchid collection began when Mrs. Henry T. Blow of the Carondelet neighborhood of South St. Louis gave specimens to Henry Shaw in 1876. Her husband had been a business leader and US congressman. President Grant, who used to deliver firewood to the Blow family before the Civil War, appointed Henry T. Blow as minister to Brazil. It was during his service in Brazil that Blow collected the orchids.

Following that initial gift in 1876, the Garden's orchid collection grew in size and prominence thanks to gifts and acquisitions. The collection features many rare and unusual specimens, and the Garden is actively building its collection of wild-sourced species.

*This photo of hundreds of potted orchid plants in Missouri Botanical Garden's collection dates to the turn of the century. (Photo courtesy of Missouri Botanical Garden.)*

The daughter of Mr. and Mrs. Henry T. Blow, Susan E. Blow, conducted an experimental kindergarten in Carondelet and then spearheaded the kindergarten movement first in St. Louis, and then across the nation.

# (c.1820)

# OLDEST HOUSE IN THE CITY
## THE CONSTANT-ARPE HOUSE
### 6717 Pennsylvania

Somewhere in the city, the oldest house is disguised by layers of siding and may be surrounded by new rooms and porches. Beneath all the modern additions, the oldest house is likely log, and probably has French traits.

A good candidate for that historic home is a little house at 6717 Pennsylvania Avenue in the Carondelet neighborhood. Though no evidence definitively proves the exact age of the home, its very structure—reflecting early French and Creole building practices—suggests its antiquity.[34]

The cottage sits atop a high stone basement. That high basement is constructed of rubble, or irregular stones like those that French settlers chiseled from the limestone bluffs along the river. In that basement, the hand-hewn log joists are visible. A hand-hewn wood sill course that rests on the rubble foundation is studded with large wooden pegs. In French style, the upper walls were braced into this wood sill course with pegs.

The house was originally one small room—also typical of the early French dwellings. French-style galleries extend the width of the front and back of the house. (The back gallery was enclosed decades ago for a kitchen and bath.)

*This photo shows 6717 Pennsylvania Avenue in the city's Carondelet neighborhood as it appeared in 1945. The bend in the rear roof, reflecting the French-style double-pitched roof, is still visible. (Photo courtesy of Carondelet Historical Society.)*

The roofline reflects a distinctive French Colonial building trait. The gabled roof of the house extends over the galleries and looks bent because the French built their roofs with two pitches. Though the front slope of the gabled roof appears to have been straightened, the slope of the roof toward the back still has a bend where the two pitches meet. Wood shingles and bark-covered braces are still visible in the porch attic.

The antiquity of the dwelling is further suggested by the name historically connected with it: Constant. Members of the Constant family moved to Carondelet from other French settlements during the Spanish Colonial Era. Leon Constant married the youngest daughter of Clement Delor De Treget, who founded the Carondelet neighborhood in 1767.

---

*Most of the earliest homes in St. Louis were located on the riverfront and razed to make room for 19th-century development. The Carondelet neighborhood, originally the French Village of Carondelet, grew slowly and experienced minimal pressure to redevelop the areas of early settlement. The result is that many of its early homes have survived.*

---

# OLDEST GREENHOUSE
## THE LINNEAN HOUSE
**Missouri Botanical Garden**

The elegant Linnean House in the Missouri Botanical Garden dates to the Victorian era, when the larger panes of glass needed to build greenhouses were more available and there was a fascination with exotic, tropical plants. Built in 1882, the Linnean House is the oldest continuously operating greenhouse west of the Mississippi.

Its 16 huge, south-facing windows gather the rays of the winter sun to naturally warm its interior. The mostly glass roof seems to fill the interior with sunlight, even on the gloomiest of winter days. Ornamental brickwork forms piers between the windows and brick corbelling at the roofline.

This historic greenhouse is one of only five structures in the Missouri Botanical Garden that dates to the life and leadership of Henry Shaw (1800–1889), the English immigrant who dedicated the fortune he made selling hardware to developing Missouri Botanical Garden and Tower Grove Park. He chose another English immigrant, architect George I. Barnett, to design the greenhouse.

Barnett, a native of Nottingham, arrived in St. Louis in 1839. He became St. Louis's premier architect in the mid-19th century and became Shaw's friend and chief architect. He designed the greenhouse as an orangery, to house citrus trees and other tropical plants over the winter. It was named in honor of Swedish

*The Linnean House as it appeared c. 1900. An authentic $1.5 million restoration of the Linnean House was completed in the winter of 2010-2011. (Photo courtesy of Missouri Botanical Garden.)*

botanist Carl Linnaeus, the creator of the naming system for plants. A bust of Linnaeus rests atop the gable end over the entrance to the greenhouse. To either side are busts of English botanist Thomas Nuttal and of American botanist Asa Gray.

The formal, symmetrical design of the brick and glass structure, topped by sculptures, is an immediate visual delight. Inside, however, is another treat for visitors. For nearly 140 winters, generations of St. Louisans anxious for spring have found the sweet scents of camelias, jasmine, and a variety of tropical plants within the walls of the Linnean House.

---

*The Piper Palm House in Tower Grove Park is a simpler predecessor to the Linnean House. Shaw commissioned Barnett to design this greenhouse in 1877; it has since been renovated as a venue for weddings and events.*

---

# OLDEST LIBRARY BUILDING
## BARR BRANCH
1701 S Jefferson Ave.

On September 17, 1906, the first St. Louis Public Library opened. Barr Branch Library, on the South Side, resulted from the generosity of two extraordinary businessmen, the passage of a tax levy, the talents of a German American architect, and a tornado.

Andrew Carnegie, the Scottish American business tycoon who amassed a fortune expanding the steel industry, donated $1 million dollars to build libraries in St. Louis. His gift required that half of the funds be used for a central library and half used for neighborhood or branch libraries. He also required that the City supply the building sites and make a commitment to provide for ongoing support of the libraries.

The citizens of St. Louis responded favorably by voting in April of 1901 to tax themselves to support a library system.

William Barr, whose St. Louis dry goods business became the Barr in Famous-Barr, donated the prominent corner lot at Jefferson and Lafayette Avenues for a new library. Carnegie was pleased with the gift of the site, calling William Barr "my dear friend" and adding in Scottish dialect, "He is a fellow Scot, and a 'wee drap bluid atween us' goes far, as you know, among Scotchmen."[35]

The corner site donated by Barr had been the site of Mount Calvary Episcopal Church. When a deadly tornado swept through the city on May 27, 1896, it destroyed the Episcopal church along with much of the Lafayette Square neighborhood. The corner lot was left vacant. (The former pastor of Mount Calvary Episcopal Church, the Reverend Benjamin E. Reed, gave the invocation at the cornerstone laying for the new library in December of 1905.)

German American architect Theodore Link, the architect of castle-like Union Station, designed the dignified brick-and-stone library building. Its restrained design reflected classical models. The new Barr Branch Library was furnished with the circulation desk and books from the Model Library in the Missouri State Building at the 1904 World's Fair.

*The Barr Branch Library as it appeared in 1927. The lines overhead powered the streetcar lines. (Photo courtesy of St. Louis Public Library.)*

After its opening, the new Barr Branch Library was immediately busy. During its first week of operation, 1,691 books were taken out, 799 by children and 892 by adults.[36]

---

*While the Barr Branch is the oldest library building, Saint Louis University's library has the oldest library book collection in the area. The beginnings of the collection date to 1829, when the Jesuit missionaries from Belgium assumed the management of what was then St. Louis College.*

---

# OLDEST *MAD MEN* FIRM
## OBATA DESIGN
**1610 Menard St.**

**B**aby boomers who breakfasted on Chex cereals, contemporary financial planners, and anyone who has enjoyed a cold Busch beer have all seen the work of Obata Design. The design and marketing team at Obata brand the communications for Emerson Electric, including the annual report for the Fortune 500 Company. They painted the Alps on the Busch beer can. And they created the artwork for cereal boxes based on Ralston-Purina's Checkerboard Square.

Obata has been branding, marketing, and creating the images for some of the nation's most iconic companies for over seven decades. This creative agency, the oldest in St. Louis, is rooted in the drive of a young woman artist and a multitalented Japanese American man in the months following the end of World War II.

In 1945, a 25-year-old illustrator for a printing company, Alice Hausner, decided to strike out on her own as a freelance artist. Within a few months, Hausner had more work than she could handle. She was joined by Kimio Obata, who had been working at the same printer. This Japanese American had spent over a year in an internment camp in Utah before he and his parents were able to come to St. Louis in 1944.

The firm founded by this creative duo not only provided abundant artwork for the famed Gardner Advertising agency, but also landed contracts with giant companies and helped develop

*A co-founder of OBATA modeled the checkered night shirt and cap for a 1955 Rice Chex photo shoot. (Photo courtesy of Chris Haller of OBATA Design.)*

their iconic images. They developed the corporate identity of Emerson and also provided them with industrial design. The artists of Obata designed the "M" logo for Monsanto and created corporate displays and award-winning multimedia presentations. Their design work included labels and bottles for Anheuser-Busch products.

The firm renovated a late 19th-century Presbyterian Mission in the Soulard area for their offices and studios in 1982. While in the historic building, it became St. Louis's first creative services firm to leap into the digital age. Obata developed web programming and video productions, and at the same time the firm developed the original sculpted version of the Bud Light mascot, Spuds MacKenzie.

*Kimio Obata's younger brother, Gyo, founded the architectural and engineering giant, Hellmuth, Obata and Kassabaum, in 1955.*

# Oldest McDonald's Restaurant

9915 Watson Road

**M**cDonald's restaurants are so much a part of the St. Louis landscape, and the national landscape, that it is hard to imagine that they could ever have been novelties. When the first McDonald's opened on Watson in 1958, however, it was not only a novelty—it seemed exotic.

The concept of McDonald's was only a decade old at that point. It originated when brothers Dick and Mac McDonald streamlined the operations of their restaurant in San Bernardino, California. They introduced their "Speedee Service System," later known as fast food, and offered a nine-item menu. The staple was the 15-cent hamburger. A native Chicagoan, Ray Kroc, who was a distributor for a milkshake mixer, was fascinated by the McDonald's concept and became their franchise agent. In 1955, he opened the first restaurant for McDonald's System, Inc., in Des Plaines, Illinois.

St. Louisan Bill Wyatt had already worked at a bakery as a bread slicer and wrapper and had driven a bread delivery route when he heard about the innovative McDonald's concept. At that time, "the nearest one was in Champaign, Illinois, so Don Kuehl [his partner] and I drove there to see it," Wyatt remembered. "We were impressed, so we drove on to Chicago and bought a franchise."[37]

The franchise cost $2,500. It took two years to find the right site, 9915 Watson, and build the eye-catching restaurant. It opened on August 30, 1958.

The very look of the small, walk-up-service restaurants served as McDonald's logo and advertisement. Two giant, neon-lit golden arches reached from the ground to far above the flat roofs of the small restaurant buildings. In a few years, these "Golden Arches" became synonymous with cheap and fast hamburgers to feed a car full of kids.

Six years later, Wyatt and Kuehl opened their second McDonald's at Gravois and Hampton. Eventually Wyatt owned 21 McDonald's. Though the original McDonald's walk-up restaurant building on Watson is long gone, a mansard roof model McDonald's operates on the original site.

---

*When the McDonald's on Watson opened, all the employees were males. That was a rule for McDonald's franchises. Wyatt noted, "I'm sure it was because he [Kroc] believed that if there were girls working, boys would start hanging around and that would create an atmosphere that might cause older customers to stay away."[38]*

---

# Oldest Shopping Mall
## South County Mall
18 S County Way

Outh County Mall opened in October of 1963 with three days of ceremonies. This suburban mall was set in the middle of a parking lot that could accommodate what seemed like an astronomical number of cars—3,000. The anchor store of the space-aged mall, Famous-Barr, was topped by a "cupola" that looked more like a UFO had just landed on the roof than an architectural feature.

The very concept of the modern shopping mall was still new when the doors opened and crowds charged in. Only seven years earlier, the first shopping mall that was fully enclosed and climate-controlled had opened in Edina, Minnesota. Soon the modern malls were expanding the idea of the suburban dream. They were popping up amongst the ranch-house subdivisions that had been spurred by VA loans across the country. In St. Louis, Northland Mall was thriving in booming North County. Early incarnations of Westroads, Crestwood Mall, and River Roads were welcoming suburban housewives when South County Mall was planned as the "Lemay Center."

The County Planning Commission rezoned the 55-acre site framed by Lindbergh Boulevard, Lemay Ferry, Union, and Forder Roads from single-family to business use in 1961. Famous-Barr, led by president Stanley J. Goodman, acted as the developer and planned and built Famous-Barr's "Store of the Future." The designer of the Greyhound Bus who became a consultant to NASA, Raymond Loewry, designed the new Famous-Barr. The store featured 200,000 square feet on two levels. The JCPenney department store was the mall's other anchor. The rest of the enclosed mall, the mid-century version of the old town Main Street, included scores of boutiques and a National Food Store. The mall's modern look was the work of Viennese-born architect Victor Gruen, who revolutionized American shopping mall design.

*Photographer Henry T. Mizuki captured this view of the then-new Famous-Barr department store in South County Mall. (Photo courtesy of Missouri Historical Society.)*

South County Mall was an immediate success, with crowds stampeding into Famous-Barr for sales. A multimillion-dollar expansion that started in 1978 added a new Stix, Baer & Fuller, and another expansion in 2001 added a Sears department store.

In recent decades, the early malls have been totally rebuilt or demolished. South County Mall, however, still stands and operates almost as a reminder of the day when the enclosed, air-conditioned mall was the suburban downtown.

---

*In 1961, moving sidewalks were under consideration for the space-age mall. Developers explained, "The moving sidewalks would be located to transport pedestrians from the parking lot to the center."[39]*

---

# 1779

# Oldest Public Market
## Soulard Market
730 Carroll St.

Soulard Market stirs images of stacks of tree-ripened peaches covering wood counters, pyramids of oranges, bins filled with russet potatoes, and sweet tomatoes in August. In summer, people buy strawberries by the case, and in fall, they buy apples by the bushel. Here the air is filled with the sounds of each transaction—whether the sale is for a small carton of blueberries or 20 pounds of Vidalia onions—conducted at 147 individual stands. Occasionally, on a hot summer afternoon, the scent from the nearby Mississippi fills the open-air market.

This marketplace is in its third century of business. Its story originated in St. Louis's earliest days as a French settlement, is linked to the French Revolution, and takes twists and turns through St. Louis history.

The market began when local farmers gathered on the flat meadow just south of the fur trading post of St. Louis to sell their fruits, vegetables, and livestock to the early settlers. That informal market was already operating when a Creole, Gabriel Cerre, received the adjacent acreage east of Broadway as a Spanish land grant after he settled here in 1780. In 1795, Cerre's daughter Julia married a refugee from the French Revolution, Antoine Soulard, for whom the market is named.

Soulard had been an officer in the French Navy and was a Royalist. He fled France when the French Revolution devolved into the Reign of Terror and many Royalists were being guillotined. After he reached Massachusetts, he heard about the French settlement of St. Louis. Traveling here by horse and keelboat, he arrived in 1794. Once here, the talented Soulard was appointed surveyor-general for the territory. He was paid in land, including the land with the market site adjoining Cerre's land. His wedding to neighbor Julia Cerre was the social event of the year in young St. Louis.

*Farmers sold produce from their circled wagons at the market as shown in this early 20th-century postcard. (Postcard courtesy of NiNi Harris.)*

After Soulard's death, his widow began subdividing their land, and she reserved two blocks to be given to the city as a public market. In 1842, the land (along with its new market buildings) was officially transferred to the City of St. Louis.

Though sales were conducted in the French language during the market's early years, the German and English languages were heard at the market stands in the 1840s. As a public market, its buildings became the community's gathering place. In January of 1861, when the nation was headed toward civil war, area residents gathered in the market's second-story meeting room. There, the great engineer James B. Eads gave a rousing speech in support of the Union. Most of the citizens at this pro-Union rally were immigrants from Germany who were dedicated to saving the United States.

Following the Civil War, immigrants from Bohemia, and then from all over Eastern Europe, settled in the area and shopped and bartered at the market on Saturdays. By 1896, the Soulard Market Mission, a Presbyterian mission that used the market's community meeting rooms, claimed the largest primary Sunday school class in the world, with over 1,000 students.

Hungarians, Romanians, Croatians, Ruthenians, Russians, Italians, and more Germans crowded the market during the early 20th century. The market buildings had been rebuilt after a tornado in 1896. The current, much larger market buildings were constructed in 1929. City architect Albert Osburg designed the expanded Soulard Market complex that covered two full city blocks. Four 100-foot-long open-air wings, under gabled roofs, sheltered stalls for independent vendors. The wings radiated from the two-story brick building, with shops on the first floor and a gym and auditorium on the second floor.

During the 1930s, the City's recreation department offered free tap-dancing classes for neighborhood children in the market's auditorium. Bohemian children took the classes, then incorporated tap dancing along with their Bohemian folk songs into their parish theatricals at nearby St. John Nepomuk Parish.

Following World War II, the Darst-Webbe housing projects were built nearby on 12th Street at Gravois. Soulard Market enabled the families at Darst-Webbe to fill their tables with healthy food at reasonable prices.

Recent decades have brought another twist to the story of Soulard Market: Young people raised in the suburbs, who have reinvigorated old city neighborhoods, relish shopping at the historic market amongst the old-timers and new immigrants from the Mideast and Asia.

---

*Decorum was maintained at Soulard Market. The market's regulations published in 1958 advised that all stand operators, as well as their employees, "shall avoid using all unduly loud, vulgar, profane, or otherwise disagreeable language."*

---

# OLDEST MUSEUM
## THE MISSOURI BOTANICAL GARDEN MUSEUM

While the nation was slowly tearing itself apart in the years leading to the Civil War, St. Louis businessman Henry Shaw was preparing his gift to generations of St. Louisans: the Missouri Botanical Garden. Shaw had been inspired by the great estate gardens he had seen on his travels in Europe. Two scientists, however, were encouraging Shaw to make his garden more than simply a botanical display. Thanks to the influence of Dr. George Engelmann and Sir William Hooker, Shaw would lay the foundation for his garden to become a great research institution by building a combined library and museum.

Engelmann was a German American who became a noted St. Louis doctor and botanist. At the urging of Engelmann, Shaw began the garden's herbarium by purchasing the collection of plant specimens of the late German Professor Johann Jakob Bernhardi. It was Hooker, the director of the Royal Botanic Gardens at Kew, who specifically encouraged Shaw to build a library and museum in the new garden. He wrote, "Very few appendages to a garden of this kind are of more importance for instruction than a library and . . . museum, and these gradually increase like a rolling snowball."[40]

Shaw responded by choosing his favorite architect, Anglo-American George I. Barnett, to design a museum for the garden. The neoclassical style museum was constructed in 1859–60 of red St. Louis brick and white Missouri limestone. The dignified building resembled the Economic Botany Museum at the Royal Botanic Gardens.

A French immigrant to St. Louis, artist Leon Pomarede covered the museum's ceiling with a colorful mural that gave the sensation of looking up through lush plant life. The Garden's original library collection was in the museum's south gallery, the herbarium, and specimens were stored and displayed in the museum's cabinets.

During the 20th century, the museum's uses included research, office space, and classrooms for children's nature classes.[41] In

2018, it was restored as the Sachs Museum, exhibiting the story of garden collections, research, and conservation here and around the world.

---

*The Missouri Botanical Garden's herbarium, which started with the 40,000 species represented in Bernhardi's herbarium, today includes 6.5 million plant specimens. One of the largest herbariums in the world, it is located in the garden's Bayer Center.*

---

*Henry Shaw commissioned fellow Englishman and architect George I. Barnett to design this combination museum and library building. (Photo courtesy of Missouri Botanical Garden.)*

# Oldest Neighborhood in St. Louis City
## The Carondelet Neighborhood

**B**efore Carondelet became the southernmost neighborhood of the City of St. Louis, it had been a French colonial-era village that eventually was chartered as the City of Carondelet. When the City of St. Louis annexed Carondelet in 1870, the community possessed a distinctive character and landscape which persist in the 21st century. Even the proportion of the streets and blocks in the earliest part of Carondelet reach back to its 18th-century French origins.

---

*The village was called Delor's Village or Louisbourg, for the French king. In 1794, the village Delor founded was officially named Carondelet in honor of the Baron de Carondelet, the governor-general of the Louisiana Territory.*

---

In 1767, only three years after St. Louis was founded, French military veteran Clement Delor de Treget and his family settled in a valley facing the Mississippi. The little three-sided valley was five miles south of the fur-trading post of St. Louis. In the valley, Delor surveyed a village along the riverbank from Bellerive

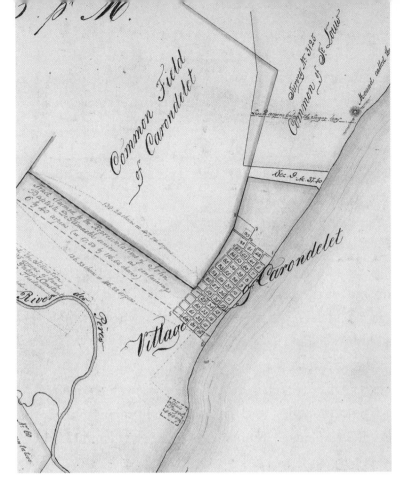

*This map shows the original village of Carondelet with its grid blocks. It was used decades later to help settle ongoing land disputes with the federal government. (Map courtesy of Missouri Department of Agriculture Land Survey Program.)*

Park south to Nagel Street. The plan for Delor's village, later named Carondelet, extended four blocks deep to current-day Michigan Avenue.

The village blocks were square, measuring 300 feet by 300 feet. In French fashion, the blocks were halved or quartered for the settlers' homes and gardens. Delor set aside a block atop the high ground for a Catholic Church.

St. Louis at this time was a frontier outpost and the center of a tremendous trading network. Fur trappers, farmers, craftsmen, merchants, and tradesman made up its population of around a thousand. At the time of the Louisiana Purchase, the farming village of Carondelet consisted of only about 250 residents living in about 50 dwellings.

The slow-growing village of Carondelet earned the status of a Town in 1832. Then new arrivals from Germany and Ireland and transplants from St. Louis began building their houses among the old Creole-inspired homes. Carondelet eventually grew to over 1,000 residents and was chartered by the state of Missouri as the city of Carondelet in 1851. New industries along Carondelet's riverfront were booming when it was annexed by neighboring St. Louis.

Despite 20th-century growth and highway construction, Delor's original street plan, the chapel eventually built on the church block, and the Creole homes scattered amongst later homes give Carondelet its unique character.

---

*Delor used the French foot to survey his village in 1767. Since the French measurement for a foot is longer than that of the English, the blocks that Delor surveyed as 300 square feet today measure 320-square-foot blocks.*

---

# Oldest Park
## Lafayette Park

**Framed by Mississippi, Missouri, Park and Lafayette Aves.**

Enchanting Lafayette Park, the centerpiece of the Victorian-era Lafayette Square neighborhood, is not only the oldest park in St. Louis—it is the oldest public park west of the Mississippi. The very idea of public parks was still new in both Europe and the United States when then-Mayor John Darby decided to set aside 30 acres for a park.

It was a hard sell to establish a park in frontier St. Louis when the city had only 12,000 residents surrounded by wilderness.

The city was about to auction some of the old St. Louis Commons, land jointly owned by St. Louisans since Spanish colonial days. The land was on high ground southwest of the St. Louis riverfront, where most of the population lived. Though he figured he would have a fight for it, Darby was determined to set aside a piece of the Commons for a park.

On March 6, 1836, Darby and Alderman Thornton Grimsley, who had made his fortune as a saddle-maker, got horses at a livery on Market Street and rode out to the Commons. They rode through the area, which was covered with an underbrush of young hickory and oak bushes, and chose the highest acreage with a view of the city in the distance.

Grimsley, who had organized and commanded "a horse-troop," thought that the future site of Lafayette Park would be "a fine

*Visitors gather at the picturesque summerhouse that was above
the grotto. (Photo courtesy of Missouri Historical Society.)*

place to maneuver his cavalry, and he proposed to call it the 'public Parade Ground.'" Darby responded that he did not care what it was called, "but that it should be kept as a park and public ground for all the people of the city of St. Louis forever."

During its early years, the land was used for military purposes. Missouri troops destined for the war with Mexico drilled in the park. At the beginning of the Civil War, the park was transformed into a dusty camp for Union volunteers.

By the end of the Civil War, however, German-trained landscape architect Maximilian Kern was guiding the development of the acreage into a delightful public park with a shaded landscape, wandering walkways, grottoes, and shimmering pools.

---

*St. Louis's first baseball teams played in Lafayette Park before the Civil War. In the 21st century, the grassy fields of Lafayette Park are the home field of both the St. Louis Perfectos and the Lafayette Square Cyclones, St. Louis's vintage baseball clubs, which play by the rules and customs of the 1860s.*

---

# OLDEST PRIVATE PLACE
## BENTON PLACE
**Lafayette Square Neighborhood**

The urban landscape of St. Louis is punctuated by private places—enclaves of impressive homes grouped around islands lush with greenery. These private places, which restrict subdividing homes and prevent commercial development, have endured as jewel-like neighborhoods of grand homes.

The evolution of the private place, beginning with Benton Place in Lafayette Square, resulted from St. Louis's booming growth in the 19th century. The city's population was doubling or even tripling during some decades. Citizens built comfortable and fashionable homes to find that in a decade or two, commercial or industrial development was encroaching. As a response to this voracious growth, Prussian-born surveyor Julius Pitzman designed the first private place, Benton Place. Pitzman's client for Benton Place was prominent attorney Montgomery Blair.

Blair platted his property facing the north gate to Lafayette Park in 1868. Pitzman, who had served as an engineer in General Sherman's army, planned a subdivision that would visually and legally protect the residential character of the neighborhood. He designed the subdivision around an oval-shaped block-long park, with the houses facing inward. The property owners owned and were responsible for both the island-like park and the streets themselves. Owning the street enabled the owners to control traffic. Deed restrictions prevented commercial development.

Stone gates, designed by Anglo-American George I. Barnett, flanked the entrance to Benton Place. By 1875, six stone-fronted townhouses with mansard roofs had already been constructed in Benton Place. Though other architectural styles would be represented in Benton Place homes, the smooth stone, Second Empire-style townhouses set the tone for the elite subdivision.

Benton Place became the model for the city's new, glamorous residential streets. By 1905, Julius Pitzman had surveyed 15 private places in the city, often called "home parks" because of their lush, arboreal settings.[42] These residential enclaves, superimposed on the grid of city streets, give St. Louis's landscape its unique texture and character.

*The entrance to Benton Place as seen through the gates of Lafayette Park. (Photo by NiNi Harris.)*

*Montgomery Blair, who platted Benton Place, served as President Lincoln's postmaster general. His brother, Frank Blair, represented St. Louis in Congress before he joined the Union Army.*

# Oldest Soul Food Diner
## Diner's Delight
1504 Compton Avenue

Nurses from Saint Louis University Hospital, programmers from Wells-Fargo, and bus drivers line up at the steam table at Diner's Delight to order an old-fashioned meatloaf plate with sides of blackeyed peas, sweet potatoes, or cabbage. Others are ordering Jack fish filet, chicken and gravy, or liver and onions. The setting is simple—diner chairs, Formica-topped tables, and beige walls. Images of then-presidential-candidate Barack Obama on his campaign visit to St. Louis hang on one wall. Photos of friends are framed on another wall. In this unadorned but comfortable setting, the Houston family has been serving old-fashioned soul food and country cooking to a growing and evolving community for over half a century.

Before the Houston family opened Diner's Delight, Louisiana native Jo Alma Houston was working as a seamstress in a sewing factory downtown. Herman Houston, a native of Tennessee, was a driver for the 7-Up bottling company. They concluded they could not put their eight children through college on their incomes and decided to open a diner. Jo Alma started going through the weekly editions of the *Thrifty Nickel*, looking for used restaurant equipment. Piece by piece, as they could afford it, they bought the equipment to operate a diner. Jo Alma opened Diner's Delight in one of three small storefronts in a building on Compton. Originally, the diner offered carryout only. The building owner operated a confectionary in the other storefronts. After seeing the Houstons' success, the owner suggested they expand to all three storefronts, which they occupy today.

When they opened, the neighborhood was home to many working-class people: "people who worked in hotels, and factory

*The Houston family hung this sign on the side of the diner in 2019 to celebrate their anniversary. (Photo by NiNi Harris.)*

workers."[43] In recent decades, the neighborhood has been rebuilt as the Gate District, with numbers of large, new homes along with a scattering of turn-of-the-century housing. The new development made the community more economically diverse.

In her 70s, Jo Alma decided it was time to retire. She called her youngest son, Greg, who was a district manager for the Parts Division of General Motors. He left GM to manage the diner. Five family members help run the diner, which has 13 full- and part-time employees. Since the Houstons opened the diner in 1969, it has expanded. A nephew has joined the business, and Greg and several family members have bought homes in the immediate neighborhood. The old-fashioned fare, however, has stayed almost the same. Greg mentions one of the few changes: "We serve catfish filet now. We used to serve the whole cat."[44]

---

*Jo Alma always made corn bread muffins from scratch. One day the oven broke down, and there was no corn bread. A customer said, "I don't care how you get it to me, I want corn bread." Jo Alma fried the corn bread, resulting in the diner's signature fried, flat (pancake-like) corn bread.*

---

# OLDEST SPICE SHOP
## THE SOULARD SPICE SHOP
The Grand Hall of Soulard Market, 730 Carroll St.

J ars of spices fill shelves that reach toward the ceiling in the Soulard Spice Shop. Glass counters are filled with containers of coriander seed and of ground coriander, 18 different kinds of pepper, three varieties of anise, and eight varieties of gourmet sea salts. Bottles of salad dressings fill baskets atop the counters. Jars of jam, boxes of teas, and bottles of flavorings are stacked on wood shelves. The experience of the Soulard Spice Shop is a sensory delight, with the aroma of Chauvin coffee beans being ground, or of an order of cinnamon sticks, basil, or dill being filled.

The small shop offers 460 varieties of spices and dried herbs, plus flavorings for sale. Orders are filled for baby boomers wanting to recreate the flavor of their grandmother's split pea and ham soup, or someone wanting the shop's signature blend "Soulard Grill" to give their barbecue special flavor. The orders measured and filled add up to 400 to 600 pounds of spices sold each week.

The spice trade involves skills that take years to learn and develop, and the proprietors of the Soulard Spice Shop—three generations of the Schmitz family—have been perfecting their skills over the last 106 years.

In 1914, German Americans Michael and Katherine Schmitz opened a grocery at 1718 S. 9th Street (only a block from the market) and lived upstairs. In their storefront grocery, the

*On the last day of World War II, German Americans Michael and Katherine Schmitz celebrated the war ending by decorating their shop window with flags and photos of their sons in uniform. Foreign-born Americans often felt a need to demonstrate their loyalty to America during both world wars. (Photo courtesy of Linda Schmitz.)*

Schmitzes roasted coffee and sold produce and spices. After the new Soulard Market buildings were constructed in 1929, the Schmitzes rented space in the Grand Hall, where their offerings included their homemade root beer.[45] At age 13, after completing seventh grade, their son Michael assumed responsibility for running the family business.

The third generation, Linda Schmitz, grew up in the trade and began working full-time at the spice shop at age 22. She bought the business from her father in 1986. Along with selling spices from around the world and having a deli with specialty cheeses and meats, Linda offers customers signature blends. The Soulard Grill blend makes everything from barbecue to vegetables enticing.

---

*Michael and Katherine Schmitz had emigrated from the Austro-Hungarian Empire in 1903. Their son Michael attended grade school at the Saints Peter and Paul Parish, the Catholic parish of the Germans in the Soulard neighborhood.*

---

# OLDEST STATUE
## STATUE OF THOMAS HART BENTON
**Lafayette Park**

Flags flew from the handsome townhouses facing Lafayette Park on May 27, 1868. Tens of thousands of people, including 3,000 public schoolchildren dressed in white and carrying red roses, gathered in the park for the unveiling of the first public monument in the entire state of Missouri. The statue memorialized adopted St. Louisan and United States Senator Thomas Hart Benton, who had served 30 years in the Senate beginning with Missouri's statehood in 1821.

This monumental leader, as a hotheaded youth, had gotten himself into trouble repeatedly. Benton had to leave his native North Carolina and then ruined his reputation in Tennessee after he shot Andrew Jackson in a brawl. After coming west to St. Louis, he practiced law and killed his courtroom adversary, attorney Charles Lucas, in a duel.

He evolved into a political leader, exchanging ideas and information with traders, fur trappers, mountain men, missionary priests, and General William Clark. As Missouri's first senator, he championed Manifest Destiny. His political evolution, from originally supporting slavery to becoming an advocate for its end, led to him losing the statewide election in 1850. Later, as a congressman, Benton spoke out against slavery.

When the state decided to honor the late Senator Benton with a statue, America's first woman professional sculptor got the job.

*The unveiling of the statue of Thomas Hart Benton. (Illustration courtesy of the Robert Campbell House Museum.)*

INAUGURATION OF THE BENTON STATUE AT ST. LOUIS, MAY 27, 1868.—SKETCHED BY A. M. STUDENT.—[SEE PAGE 356.]

Harriet Hosmer was a Massachusetts native who first came to Missouri to study anatomy at McDowell's Medical College.

Since the outdoors diminished the human figure, Hosmer created a 10-foot-tall statue of Benton, placed atop a granite pedestal. Avoiding the artistic cliché of portraying politicians in tails making a speech with an outstretched arm, Hosmer portrayed the intense-looking Benton wearing his long cloak and carrying a rolled map, presumably a map of the American West. The bronze statue was cast by Ferdinand von Miller's Royal Foundry in Munich.

Benton's daughter, Jesse Benton Fremont, touchingly described the moment the statue was revealed. "As the veil fell away from the statue, its bronze gilded with the warm sunshine, the children threw their roses at its base."[46]

---

*Though President Andrew Jackson carried Benton's bullet in his arm until his death, the two eventually became political allies. Benton was described as a "Jacksonian Democrat."*

---

# (1920s–1960s)
# OLDEST COMMERCIAL STREET
## CHEROKEE STREET
**From Jefferson Ave. to Compton Ave.**

From World War I through the 1960s, business districts like Cherokee Street and North 14th Street were meccas where neighborhood shoppers could find everything from shoes to fresh-baked bread, to housewares, to a haircut or furniture.

During the late 1950s and early 1960s, Saturdays for the Hohn family of South St. Louis were spent on Cherokee Street. Pat, along with her sisters, mother, and grandmother, walked the mile from their home to Cherokee. Once there, they stopped at Fairchild's Dry Goods, where her grandmother bought pillowcases and tablecloths with embroidery designs "stamped" on them. Then she examined all the shades of embroidery thread for sale. After that, they explored all the dime stores and variety stores. Dishes, knickknacks, and kitchenware were stacked from floor to ceiling along the narrow aisles of Morris Variety. Pat's mother bought their clothes at the "big" JCPenney or at Worth's ladies' clothing. Of all the shoe stores, Proper Shoe was the best-known. The proprietor always "gave" the toddlers their first pair of shoes when they started walking. They were white high-tops.

During the early 1960s, the glamorous new suburban malls drew shoppers away from the charming old commercial streets lined with brick and terra-cotta stores. Some once-

*The Switzerland Creamery and Cut Price Grocery at 2610 Cherokee as it appeared in the 1930s. (Photo courtesy of Missouri Historical Society.)*

thriving districts slowly faded and then disappeared. Other historic commercial streets, like South Grand, the Loop, and Euclid Avenue, were reinvented as delightful dining and entertainment destinations.

After much struggle, Cherokee Street is reviving not just for diners, but also as an old-fashioned commercial street. Gardeners are still buying bedding plants on the corner of Cherokee and Compton as they have for 60 years. Neighbors still walk to a barber or salon for a haircut. Many of the new shops that are reenergizing Cherokee as a commercial district, however, have a distinctive Latin American flair. For years, the old German bake shop has been home to a Mexican bakery. Mexican groceries and butchers fill old shops. A piñata, a first communion dress, cowboy hats, and leather boots are all available in Cherokee Street stores. And where Germans did the polka to accordion music, shoppers stop for Mexican cuisine.

---

*During the fifties, Favorite Bakery sold German-style danishes, stollens, and coffee cakes by the hundreds. The baker filled a big laundry basket with dollar bills, the profits from the day, to carry to the bank.*

---

# WEST

# OLDEST BILLIARDS HALL
## ST. LOUIS UNIVERSITY HIGH SCHOOL
4970 Oakland Avenue

S t. Louis University High School is recognized throughout the region as an outstanding educational institution that graduates young men prepared to shape the future. Its campus on Oakland also happens to have the oldest billiards hall in St. Louis.

The high school shares its roots with Saint Louis University and was founded as "an academy for young gentlemen"[47] on the St. Louis riverfront in 1818—making it the oldest high school in St. Louis. During the 19th and early 20th centuries, the high school shared the campus of the university, first downtown and later at the Midtown campus at Grand and Lindell Boulevards. After the turn of the century, the Midtown campus was growing more crowded.

In 1922, construction began for a separate campus for the high school on Oakland Avenue just west of Kingshighway. An independent high school campus in an ideal location opposite Forest Park was possible because of a half-million-dollar gift from Mrs. Anna F. Backer. Her late husband's family had made a fortune in the milling industry, having started with nothing more than a wheelbarrow.

The new, three-story brick high school was designed by Barnett, Haynes & Barnett, the architects of the great Cathedral on Lindell. For the school, they chose the English Gothic style with its tapestry

1023:— St. Louis University High School, St. Louis, Mo.

*The English Gothic style St. Louis University High School as shown in a 1920s postcard. (Postcard courtesy of NiNi Harris.)*

of brick embellished with "blue Bedford stone." In addition to the 29 classrooms, the school boasted a large reference library and a chapel.

In 1944, the Father's Club and the Jesuit faculty decided a recreation room for use in bad weather was needed. They excavated a new basement and used the excavated dirt to level the sports fields. The new basement recreation area carried an estimated price tag of $25,000.

When the project was started, billiards was a popular activity. Over 80 billiards rooms operated in St. Louis, and many clubs and organizations offered a table for play. The new recreation room provided billiards for students. While billiards rooms faded from the sporting landscape, St. Louis University High School continues to maintain its billiards room. More than 50 billiards tables are available to students for play before and after the school day.

*The new basement floor for indoor recreation offered something that is shocking today—a senior smoker area. Until smoking was banned, that entire corner of the basement was filled with smoke most of the time.*

# OLDEST BOWLING ALLEY
## SARATOGA LANES
2725 Sutton Ave.

German immigrants brought their lager beer, pretzels, gymnastics, and a love of bowling with them to St. Louis. And a lot of Germans came to St. Louis. In 1900, German immigrants who called St. Louis home numbered almost 59,000. And that did not include the tens of thousands of second- and third-generation German Americans who enjoyed German foods, music, and sports.

Catering to all these Germans, tavern owners installed bowling alleys in their basements or back rooms. To keep Mr. Stockstrom home and away from the alleys with their sometimes seedy inhabitants, Mrs. Stockstrom had a bowling alley constructed in the basement of their new "Magic Chef" Mansion.[48] Some German congregations even built their own bowling alleys as part of their church complexes. Between 1910 and 1920, twenty new bowling alleys were built in St. Louis. Saratoga Lanes was one of those new alleys.

The owner of the Maplewood Planing Mill, Albert Carl Blood, opened his Saratoga Lanes on the second floor of a new Maplewood office building in 1916. This "second floor" alley symbolically raised the respectability of the game by attracting a "new" crowd of bowlers. Saratoga Lanes offered league play and encouraged women to bowl at their lanes. Saratoga Lanes

*The home of Saratoga Lanes dates to 1916. (Photo by NiNi Harris.)*

was one of the first bowling alleys in the country to offer both women's leagues and mixed-league play.

Though the wooden gutters are original, a 1950s renovation gave the place a new feel, which slowly became a "retro" look. "The wood-and-metal ball returns swoop and curve with a 1950s Sputnik vibe, as do the turquoise and white fiberglass benches and the chrome ashtrays and beverage holders hooked behind them."[49] The 1950s automatic pinsetters and ball returns eliminated the need for the traditional "pin boy."

Saratoga Lanes claims to be the oldest bowling alley west of the Mississippi.

---

*The last remaining parish-operated bowling alley, Epiphany Lanes at 3164 Ivanhoe Avenue, opened around 1950. The young men of the parish served as the pin boys, until an automatic pinsetter was installed around 1990.*

---

# OLDEST COFFEE ROASTER
## RONNOCO COFFEE
618 South Boyle Ave.

Coffee, a luxury during the early days of St. Louis, had to be hauled by keelboat from New Orleans. Once river traffic was steam-powered, paddle wheelers regularly delivered shipments of coffee from New Orleans. The waves of German and Eastern-European immigrants, arriving after their failed revolutions in 1848, brought their Viennese coffeehouse traditions with them. Soon coffee was a staple not only for St. Louisans, but also for the St. Louis economy.

St. Louis became a major receiving and distribution center for coffee during the mid-19th century. Brokers worked with growers to send coffee directly to St. Louis. Local companies roasted—and sometimes ground, packaged, and shipped—St. Louis–brand coffees. The coffee that cowboys drank around the

*This small commercial roaster is typical of turn-of-the-century equipment that roasted 20 to 75 pounds of whole bean coffee. (Photo by NiNi Harris.)*

campfire, that miners drank in frontier rooming houses, and that farmwives served in sod houses came from St. Louis. New coffee companies grew up during the early 20th century.

At the 1904 World's Fair, two brothers, J.P. and James O'Connor, were introduced to imported coffee beans roasted over a gas flame. Inspired by this innovation in coffee roasting, they started their own coffee company, delivering their gas-roasted coffee beans to local hotels by horse-drawn buggy. They named their coffee company by spelling their own name backwards: Ronnoco.

In 1919, the O'Connor brothers sold the company to the Guyol family, who continued to expand the business. With recent expansions, Ronnoco supplies convenience stores, offices, and hotels in 41 states. In addition to coffee, Ronnoco supplies teas, hot chocolate, smoothies, cups, flavoring syrups, and condiments.

---

*The seductive aroma of coffee beans often floats through the air near Boyle and Highway 40, St. Louis's new coffee district. The facilities of Ronnoco Coffee and Thomas Coffee are on South Boyle near Highway 40, and Kaldi's Coffee is to the east at 3983 Gratiot Street.*

---

# Oldest Hospital Building
## Barnes Hospital
### 1 Barnes Jewish Hospital Plaza

Tucked behind the modern high-rise hospital buildings along Kingshighway, the old Barnes Hospital building from 1914 stands in the shadows. That hospital building was the seed of one of the nation's outstanding research hospital complexes—Barnes-Jewish Hospital.

It was named for the business wizard who donated the money to build the hospital, Robert Augustus Barnes. Born in Washington, DC, in 1808, he was orphaned at age 13. After living with an uncle in Kentucky and working as a clerk, Barnes came to St. Louis in 1830. The clerk started his own grocery business, and from that humble beginning, he entered the railroad industry and the then-huge, local sugar-refining industry. Eventually, Barnes became president of the Bank of the State of Missouri, even lending money to a young Adolphus Busch to start a brewery. When Robert Barnes passed away in 1892, two years after his wife, he was a very wealthy man with no heirs.

Barnes had designated $1 million from his estate be used to build "a modern general hospital for sick and injured persons without distinction of creed." By 1912, Barnes's estate had increased to more than $2 million. At that time, trustees of the estate bought property on Kingshighway Boulevard near Forest

*Barnes Hospital had grown substantially by the time this postcard was printed in the 1930s. (Postcard courtesy of NiNi Harris.)*

Park and hired the renowned architect Theodore Link to design the hospital building.

Before ground was ever broken for the building, the Barnes trustees negotiated an agreement with Robert Brookings of the Washington University Board of Trustees to make this new "Barnes Hospital" the teaching hospital for the university's school of medicine. Knowing of this affiliation, Link added numerous laboratories, exam rooms, and operating rooms to the hospital's design. Barnes Hospital opened on December 7, 1914, with 250 beds and 26 patients.

The growing hospital merged with Jewish Hospital in 1996, combining and expanding their services and research capabilities. A century after the old Barnes Hospital was built on Kingshighway, patients travel from around the world to seek treatment at Barnes-Jewish Hospital.

---

*German American architect Theodore Link, the architect of the original Barnes Hospital building, is best known for designing St. Louis's castle-like Union Station.*

---

# OLDEST HUNT CLUB
## BRIDLESPUR HUNT
125 Valley Green Lane

The Busch family had a golden touch and a common touch. Family members were flamboyant, full of bluster, dripped money, and were generous. Other immigrant families viewed the Busch family with pride as fellow immigrants who had made good. All those characteristics made this extraordinary family less attractive to the city's old money.

The Busch family also loved riding, shooting, and hunting. By establishing the Bridlespur Hunt Club, the extended Busch family, including the Orthwein branch, could enjoy their favorite sports while creating their own social world.

*Activities and exhibitions at Horse Shows during the 1930s at the Bridlespur Hunt club. (Photo courtesy of Missouri Historical Society.)*

The glamorous and colorful first hunt at Bridlespur, originally in Huntleigh Village, was held in May 1928. The men wore pink coats with robin's-egg blue collars, white jodhpurs, and black velvet hunting caps. The ladies' dress included silk hats with mesh veils.

Gussie Busch spent considerable time at Bridlespur fox hunting—riding horses with a pack of hounds chasing wild game across the countryside, known as "riding to hounds." Through the decades, riding and hunting at Bridlespur have continued uninterrupted. Even during World War II, the hounds still went out twice a week.

The original location of Bridlespur was on present-day Squires Lane. The club's original steeplechase course overlaps the site of Plaza Frontenac. By the mid-1950s, continued development in west St. Louis County forced the club to move. New kennels, a clubhouse, and a skeet-shooting range were opened in 1957 at a new site in St. Charles County, west of Weldon Spring and the Busch Wildlife Area. In 2006, development once again forced the club to move, this time to 1,400 acres of property in Lincoln County.[50]

In addition to foxhunting, Bridlespur sponsors numerous other activities, including the annual Bridlespur Charity Horse Show, schooling shows, hunter paces, and hunter trials, all open to the public. Their facilities are available to other organizations to enjoy horse-related activities.

---

*Bridlespur members still wear pink hunting coats. Pink tails are the signature attire for formal events at the Bridlespur Hunt Club.*

---

# Oldest Reform Jewish House of Worship

## Temple Israel

1 Rabbi Alvan D. Rubin Dr.

A t the dedication of the New Temple Israel on September 7, 1962, civic leader and Rabbi Ferdinand Issermann noted that St. Louis was the largest metropolitan area of Reform Judaism in the world.[51] This third home of Temple Israel is the oldest building constructed as a house of worship for Reform Jews in St. Louis. It is also the oldest house of worship that is still home to its original Jewish congregation.[52]

Temple Israel's Creve Coeur site, chosen in the mid-1950s, covered nearly 24 acres at the corner of Ladue and Spoede Roads. The firm of Hellmuth, Obata, and Kassabaum was only four years old when they designed the new complex for the congregation. Their design featured a combined auditorium and sanctuary building that had a hexagon-shaped footprint. It was linked to distinct chapel and education buildings. The estimated cost for the complex in the campus-like setting was over $2 million. The final house of worship was more restrained than the original plans, which had featured a roof that formed a series of peaks, had proposed. The simplified lines of the completed Temple Israel exemplified mid-century modern design, with its cream-colored brick walls contrasting dramatically with the lush green lawns and trees of the surrounding acres.

The historic congregation was founded in 1886 by members who had broken off from Shaare Emeth. After meeting in a theatre building, they moved into their first house of worship just west of downtown at Pine and Leffingwell Streets. Their first rabbi, Solomon H. Sonnenschein, a native of Slovakia, was a leading spokesman for Reform Judaism. He gave his sermons in German and in English and attracted a following among Christians. Rabbi Leon Harrison, a native of Liverpool, England who was educated in New York, became the congregation's second rabbi in 1891. He was an inspiring speaker who also developed a Christian following. Under his leadership, "Temple Israel became one of the leading Reform Jewish congregations in America."[53]

The congregation built a monumental house of worship on Holy Corners, at Washington Avenue and Kingshighway Boulevard, in 1907. Modeled after a Roman temple with Corinthian columns, this second home of Temple Israel was surrounded by other great institutions. At the dedication of their house of worship in its prominent location, the president of the congregation stated, "No longer as in dark Europe need we hide our sanctuaries in obscure alleys, or skulk timidly in ghettos."[54]

In 1929, Rabbi Ferdinand Issermann succeeded Harrison and like his predecessors became a leader for the greater St. Louis community. He preached about the threat to Jews in Europe following his trips to Germany after the Nazi takeover in 1933. During his 35-year tenure as rabbi, Issermann initiated successfully integrated programs.

Following World War II, St. Louis's Jewish population was moving to the suburbs. By 1962, 70 percent of Temple Israel's congregation lived in St. Louis County. Issermann helped dedicate the new house of worship in Creve Coeur, nearer the homes of the congregation.

---

*Many former Jewish houses of worship have been used as churches and others as venues for arts organizations. The home of the B'nai El congregation constructed in the Shaw neighborhood in 1905, however, was renovated as the Temple Apartments.*

---

# Oldest Kosher Butcher and Deli

## Kohn's Kosher Restaurant, Deli and Meat Market
### Old Olive Street Road

O ff of Olive Street Road, in an area where the Schnucks, Dierbergs, and Aldi stores now command much of the market for kosher foods, the atmosphere in Kohn's Kosher Deli is intimate. In the midst of suburban shopping strip malls, Kohn's Deli is reminiscent of the shops of St. Louis's old Orthodox Jewish neighborhoods from the turn of the 20th century. Those shops, with their signs in Yiddish, were in the tenement- and factory-packed neighborhoods just north of downtown St. Louis. At Kohn's in Creve Coeur, conversations in Yiddish are overheard as pastrami sandwiches are made completely kosher, of locally sourced meats. From matzo ball soup to Asian salad with salmon, to tabbouleh (a flavorful Levantine vegetarian salad), everything is approved by Vaad Hoeir of St. Louis.[55]

A rack filled with trays of glistening, golden brown, braided bread is rolled from the kitchen to the bakery. The bakery cases contain triangular pocket cookies filled with fruits and nuts called hamantash. There is a shelf of rugelach, a crescent-shaped pastry rolled around sweet fillings.

Above the bakery cases hangs a large black-and-white photo of a handsome young couple—Simon and Lenke "Bobbie" Kohn.

*Kohn's Kosher Deli is known as the home of the "Killer Pastrami Sandwich." (Photo by NiNi Harris.)*

The photo was taken in Germany, staged outdoors under trees, a few years before the couple immigrated to the United States in 1949. Bobbie was originally from Hungary and Simon from Boleslawiec, Poland, near the German border. He was rounded up by the Nazis at the beginning of the war. After surviving being interred at six concentration camps, Simon met Bobbie, his brother's fiancée, in a Displaced Persons camp. After his brother was killed by Polish nationalists in 1946, Simon followed Jewish tradition and married Bobbie.

With the assistance of the Jewish Family & Children's Service, the Kohns moved to St. Louis. Mr. Kohn's first local job was as a deliveryman for Yankel Margul, who owned a store on what was then Easton Avenue (now Martin Luther King Avenue).

Both Simon and Bobbie began making homemade kosher delicacies including knishes, kreplach, strudel, khishka, and more. In 1963, they opened their own kosher deli in University City. Their 1976 move to Old Olive Street Road in Creve Coeur followed the migration of the Jewish community.

In the late 1970s, their children, Rosemary and Lenny, joined the business and expanded the deli. Kohn's deli continues as the only independent kosher butcher in the St. Louis area.

---

*From the neighborhood around the old Biddle Street Market just north of downtown, the center of the Jewish community moved west over the next century. In 1985, the editor of the* St. Louis Jewish Light *pinpointed Interstate 270 and Olive Boulevard, near Kohn's Deli, as the center of the Jewish community[56]*

---

# OLDEST SKATING RINK
## STEINBERG RINK

Forest Park

A t age 63, the Mark C. Steinberg Skating Rink is still the largest outdoor ice skating rink in the Midwest. Steinberg Rink has been described as 27,600 square feet of frozen fun, and much of that fun can be attributed to the setting. At Steinberg, people skate beneath the stars in a 1,300-acre park, with the silhouettes of bare branches of mighty trees set against the sky. The setting is so exhilarating at Steinberg that even the parents, who sit around a firepit sipping hot chocolate, enjoy waiting while their children skate.

*In fifties' style, the long, low design of the clubhouse behind the rink hugs the ground. (Photo courtesy of Missouri Historical Society.)*

The million-dollar rink was built thanks to a donation from the Mark C. Steinberg Charitable Trust. His widow had admired a rink she had seen in New York's Central Park and offered that her husband's charitable trust would pay two-thirds of the cost of a rink in Forest Park. The City used proceeds from a 1944 bond issue intended to improve parks for the remaining cost of the ice rink.

A site in the southeastern corner of the park was chosen for the rink, since it was near the excellent Kingshighway bus line. Frank Hamig was chosen as the engineer and Frederick Dunn as the architect.

A native of Minnesota who had studied architecture at Yale, Dunn helped shape the modern movement in St. Louis. In partnership with Charles Nagel, he designed the extraordinary St. Mark's Episcopal Church. After World War II, Dunn's designs for the headquarters of the National Council of State Garden Clubs and for Steinberg Rink earned acclaim.

Steinberg's clubhouse, with space for lockers, skate rentals, and a cafe, was a low, sprawling building. Its expansive glass wall is framed with gray stone walls that seem to drift into the landscape.

When the rink opened on November 11, 1957, the entrance fee was fifty cents. The opening-day crowd numbered 2,600, mostly children.

---

*While serving in the Navy during World War II, Frederick Dunn, the architect of Steinberg Rink, helped design the interiors of submarines at naval bases in Philadelphia and Houston.*

---

# OLDEST JEWISH HOUSE OF WORSHIP
## U. CITY SHUL
700 North and South Road

The striking facade of U. City Shul forms a two-tiered sweeping curve of light-yellow brick. Its mid-century modern design features "outer walls and roof converging in the sanctuary, with the altar as a focal point," according to George McCue, who was chronicling contemporary design in religious architecture in 1957.[57]

Though many of the former Jewish houses of worship that dot the city and inner suburbs are much older, the oldest building constructed as a Jewish house of worship that is still home to a Jewish congregation is the synagogue at 700 North and South Road in University City.

This synagogue is the work of architect Benjamin Shapiro, the son of Yiddish-speaking immigrants from Russia. His father was a carpenter. After graduation from Central High School in 1916, Shapiro studied architecture at the University of Illinois. Early in his career, he designed the art deco-style gates to Mount Sinai Cemetery. His works include apartment buildings with an art deco flair and the modern-style Ferguson City Hall.

He designed this house of worship for the Chesed Shel Emeth congregation in 1950. The historic roots of this congregation

*The striking contemporary design of U. City Shul immediately attracted attention. (Photo courtesy of the Missouri Historical Society.)*

date back to 1888, when a small group of Russian immigrants established a much-needed synagogue and burial society. The Shul was the home of the chief rabbis of the United Orthodox Jewish Community and was located at the intersection of Euclid Avenue and Page Boulevard in 1919. In 1950, the Chesed Shel Emeth Society in St. Louis acquired the land in University City on North and South Road to build a new synagogue.

After several decades and following a westward movement of the Jewish community, the membership began aging and declining rapidly. The congregation closed in 1996. "Through

the combined efforts of two visionary leaders, Rabbi Elazar Grunberger and Mr. Charlie Deutsch, new life was breathed into the building, re-establishing it as an outreach Shul catering to all segments of the community."[58] In 2009, it was named the U. City Shul.

---

*The Chesed Shel Emeth Society formed in 1888 by Jews who had fled the murderous pogroms in Russia, established the cemetery at 7550 Olive Boulevard. Later, the Society formed the Chesed Shel Emeth congregation.*

---

# Oldest Family-Owned Tavern
## Failoni's Restaurant and Bar
**6715 Manchester**

Posters of the Rat Pack and an enlarged print of a young Frank Sinatra's mug shot decorate the walls in this family-owned tavern. "Uncle Alex does a good Sinatra," Joey Meiners, a fourth-generation member of the Failoni family, says as he serves bottles of beer with old-style, thick burgers. On Thursday and Friday nights, in between the beers and pizza, a regular will perform an aria by Giacomo Puccini or a family member will burst into a Sinatra favorite. People have been singing regularly at Failoni's for close to 40 years, according to Rosetta, Joey's mom and a member of the third generation of the Failoni family. (Everyone seems to introduce themselves by explaining their place in the family tree.) The family has operated Failoni's on Manchester for over a century.

Before the Failoni family started serving beer at 6715 Manchester, Irish American James E. Muldoon was the proprietor of a saloon in the building for at least a decade. (The saloon is on the edge of the Dogtown neighborhood, which had been home to many Irish steelworkers.)

In 1916, Alex and Rose Failoni bought the storefront from the Lemp Brewery family. Nothing is square about the building because it fits the odd-shaped lot. So the turn-of-the-century

*The name Failoni's is carved into the old wood screen door of the family-owned tavern. (Photo by NiNi Harris.)*

tavern building and its rooms are shaped like trapezoids. The Failonis paid $12,000 for the brick, two-story building.

Alex Failoni was born in Northern Italy sometime around 1888 and immigrated to America in 1901. He first settled in Louisiana, where he met and married the Louisiana-born daughter of Italian immigrants, Rose. Their saloon on Manchester was popular with the workers at Scullin Steel, which covered blocks of the opposite side of Manchester. The steelworkers, many of whom were Irish, enjoyed beer and chili at Failoni's.

The Failoni family weathered Prohibition by selling soda and ice cream at their longtime saloon, and Alex worked as a "steel chipper" in the steel industry. The family lived in the second-floor flat over the saloon turned ice-cream parlor.

With the end of Prohibition in 1933, the family tavern was selling beer again. Eventually two of their four sons, Joe and Frank, became co-owners of Failoni's. Later Alex Jr. and Victor Failoni ran the family bar.

The family has continually expanded Failoni's. On a summer evening, with 140 people packed in the tent-covered beer garden strung with lights, Joey Meiners explains that their customers come from "North County, West County, and down the street."

---

*The signs on Failoni's date to various eras, including an old painted sign on the second-story wall that still boasts that the establishment is "air conditioned."*

---

# Oldest Irish Pub
## The Pat Connolly Tavern
6400 Oakland Ave.

E ven more than the dark-stained wood of the booths and bar (a signature of Irish pubs), and the fiddle, harp, or banjo music that floats through Pat Connolly's on some Friday nights, there is something about this Dogtown landmark that gives it the feel of an old Irish pub. It is the family atmosphere created when a white-haired, 70-year-old woman is served before the fashionable millennial.

The story of this Irish bar began in 1927, when a young Pat Connolly left his home in Dunmore, County Galway, for St. Louis. He arrived at the end of a massive wave of Irish immigration to this city that had begun with the Irish famine in the 1840s. Irish Catholic parishes still dotted much of the North Side. The jobs at Scullin Steel on Manchester had attracted many Irish to the Dogtown neighborhood south of Forest Park. At that time, St. Louis's many Irish saloons, along with the German and Bohemian pubs, had been closed by Prohibition.

After working hard to earn money at various jobs here for 15 years, Connolly and his wife Mary Ellen opened The Pat Connolly Tavern in a building at 6400 Oakland Avenue. The early-20th-century corner storefront had served as a confectionary and medical office for years before Connolly opened his bar and started serving Griesedieck beer in 1942. During the years following the war, Connolly remodeled the bar,

*This photo dates to about 70 years ago, after Pat Connolly remodeled his Dogtown neighborhood tavern and added the art deco back bar. (Photo courtesy of Joe Jovanovich.)*

but he kept or recycled now-historic features—the bar paneled with patterned wood, the art deco back bar with a circular mirror and cylinder-shaped lights, and the old-fashioned wood booths. Families packed those booths.

Through the years, other Irishmen and friends of the Connolly family—Tom McDermott and then Joe Finn—have owned and operated the tavern. Since 2015, descendants of Pat Connolly again own and manage the tavern. His daughter Teresa and grandson Joe Jovanovich maintain the atmosphere and traditions started by Pat Connolly from County Galway.

---

*When The Pat Connolly Tavern switched to Anheuser-Busch Brewery, the Griesedieck signs were replaced with a neon Budweiser marquee over the remodeled entrance. That old sign is now a rarity.*

---

# OLDEST ITALIAN TAVERN
## MILO'S BOCCE GARDEN
5201 Wilson Ave.

T he friendly sounds of Milo's—20-year-olds to 80-year-olds arguing over sports teams, ordering another beer, cheering one another on the bocce court—recall the old-time taverns that once dotted St. Louis neighborhoods. They were family-friendly, knew their customers, and their barkeeps would fill a small bucket with beer for children who were picking it up for their papas. With a few changes (for example, television screens showing sports competitions have replaced accordion music), Milo's on The Hill has maintained that enjoyable environment for over a century.

The tavern building dates to the era when the Anheuser-Busch Brewery was constructing and outfitting saloons to lease to Irish, German, and Italian immigrants who had agreed to sell their brews. The brewery also acquired the liquor licenses for taverns. Anheuser-Busch built the handsome storefront with an apartment on the second floor in 1905.

By 1908, Italian immigrant Louis Merlo was the proprietor of a tavern or saloon in the storefront. He had emigrated in 1899 and married Theresa, 10 years his junior. Louis and Theresa raised their nine children over the saloon.

The Busch family and their businesses were absorbing financial losses, first with anti-German sentiments stirred by World War I and then with Prohibition erasing their brewing industry. The brewery was selling property. By 1930, the Merlos owned their

*Louis "Forchette" Merlo (owner of Merlo's Tavern, now Milo's) stands behind his buddies (L-R): Joe "Zeek-Zeek" Zarinelli, Angelo "Chippy" Marnati, Louis "Slim" Ranzini, Henry "Chick" Pedroli, Father Charles Koester, and Mike "Herrin" Calcaterra. (Photo courtesy of Carol Ranzini Stelzer.)*

tavern and home at 5201 Wilson. During Prohibition, Louis Merlo was listed as a merchant in the "soft drinks" business.

Louis was a deeply religious man, and according to neighborhood lore, he attended 6:00 a.m. Mass each morning before opening the bar. "During slack times in the bar, he would pray the rosary," according to George Venegoni. In recording the neighborhood memories of the Italian barkeeper, Venegoni stated that "he would not tolerate foul language inside the tavern."

After Louis passed away in 1948, his widow and children managed the tavern into the 1950s. Other residents of The Hill then owned and managed the tavern, known for a time as Wil-Mar Lounge for its location at the corner of Wilson and

Marconi. Tom Savio and Joe Calcaterra changed the name to Milo's when they bought the business in the mid-1970s. In 1989, Joseph Vollmer and Tom Savio became partners in operating the historic tavern.

The duo of Volmer and Savio added to the distinctive Italian atmosphere when they built the popular bocce courts under a canopy in the garden.

---

*Though the family-run business was named Merlo's Tavern, it was commonly known as "Forchette's."*

---

# OLDEST LIVE THEATRE
## THE MUNY OPERA
Forest Park

A group of St. Louis volunteers and civic leaders decided to offer great entertainment under the stars in the sylvan setting of Forest Park. They determined to present "Light opera, by all means . . . The more elaborate, the better . . . Something spectacular . . . Something majestic and impressive . . . Lots of scenery . . . Lots of movement . . . Dancing choruses . . . Song."[59]

That was in 1919, and during its 101 seasons, attendance at the Muny Opera has numbered 55,389,828. Of its 10,700 seats, 1,456 are free seats. At this live theater, St. Louisans have witnessed the whole evolution of American musical theater from opera, to light operettas by Sigmund Romberg, Victor Herbert and Franz Lehar; to early musicals like Jerome Kern's *Showboat* that married serious subjects with spectacle; to the works of the great Rodgers and Hammerstein, from *South Pacific* to *The Sound of Music*; to the revolutionary musicals of Andrew Lloyd Weber. Audiences saw outstanding performances, some by famed stars like a young Cary Grant, and others legends like Yul Brynner in *The King and I*. And some of the young audience members (who benefitted from the free seats) grew up to become Broadway stars, including Ken Page and Norbert Leo Butz, who has won two Tony Awards.

The concept of the Muny Opera dates to before its musical mission was defined. In 1914, a theatrical celebration of the 150th anniversary of St. Louis's founding was staged on Art Hill. *The*

*The cover for the Muny's 1935 program featured trendy art deco design. (Brochure courtesy of NiNi Harris.)*

*Pageant and Masque* boasted a cast of thousands entertaining hundreds of thousands. Two years later, a committee of civic leaders marked the 300th anniversary of the death of Shakespeare with an outdoor presentation of the Bard's comedy, *As You Like It*. Since the scale of Art Hill would have overwhelmed the production, a volunteer committee surveyed Forest Park for the best setting. "They came upon a glade at the foot of a hillside.

On either side of the level area, which might serve as a stage, stood a majestic oak tree. Back beyond flowed the River des Peres through a beautiful forest. . . . Upon that hillside could be built the seats for the audience."[60] That glade and hillside became the site of the Muny Opera.

The development of the idyllic location for an outdoor theater began in 1917, thanks to the St. Louis Advertising Club. The club planned to produce Verdi's *Aida* for their international convention to be held in St. Louis. They dedicated $5,000 to improving the Forest Park site for the outdoor production. The city matched the money to help create a permanent amphitheater setting.

After the improvements were completed, the city comptroller is said to have shaken his head and mused: "They wanted a concrete pavement at the top of that hill. All right, that's fine. But this is the first time I ever saw so much concrete roll down a hillside in perfect tiers!"[61] The Advertising Club's production of *Aida* was another great success, and left the city with a permanent facility.

St. Louis was peopled by immigrants and the children of immigrants. The United States had entered the world war, and many foreign-born St. Louisans whose ancestral homelands had become enemy countries felt a need to publicly declare their patriotism. On July 4 through 7 in 1918, the new amphitheater provided a site for a great pageant called "Fighting for Freedom." This patriotic production, encouraged by President Woodrow Wilson, included audience members participating in the Pledge of Allegiance.

The first full season at the Muny was presented in the summer of 1919, after the Armistice had ended World War I. The new Municipal Theater Association, which financed productions by subscriptions of members of the Association and charged admission fees to offset the expenses, offered an eight-week season. The season included productions of John Philip Sousa's *El Capitan* and Gilbert and Sullivan's *Mikado*.

During its 101 seasons, the Municipal Theater Association has continually enhanced the setting with Works Progress Administration projects and generous donations from individuals and corporate citizens. As a result, an elegant neoclassical arcade built in 1939 frames the theater. Hillside gardens surround the facility. Even the walkways leading the Muny—tree-lined and crossing bridges over lagoons—add to the delightful experience.

---

*The massive stage, with a giant turntable, was spectacularly renovated as part of a multi-million-dollar renovation of the whole complex, funded entirely by donations.*

---

# OLDEST MOVIE THEATRE
## THE HI-POINTE
1005 McCausland Ave.

Scores of movie houses dotted St. Louis neighborhoods when the Hi-Pointe Movie Theatre opened in 1922. The new movie house was built on top of a natural ridge at the western edge of the city, where Clayton Road and McCausland Avenue intersect. The 500-seat Hi-Pointe was designed to help meet the tremendous demand to see silent movies featuring beauties like Mary Pickford and Lilian Gish, swashbucklers like Douglas Fairbanks, Sr., and actor-comedians like Buster Keaton and Charlie Chaplin.

During the first decades of the 20th century, silent movies had captured the imagination of Americans, and of St. Louisans. By 1914, the city's license collector's office reported that more than 150 neighborhood theaters were doing business. They were listed as tents, airdomes, and houses. Many of those early movie houses were in converted stores, storerooms, vaudeville theaters, and even in a former Presbyterian mission. The "airdomes" were often vacant city lots adjacent to the movie houses that were converted to outdoor venues in summer. By the time the Hi-Pointe opened in 1922, the Family Theatre on the Hill, the Melvin in Dutchtown, the Red Wing in Carondelet, the Shaw in the Shaw neighborhood, the Bridge on Natural Bridge Boulevard, and the Baden on North Broadway were presenting "moving pictures" to thousands of neighborhood residents each week.

The 1920s saw a boom in the construction both of buildings designed to be neighborhood movie houses (like the Columbia on the Hill, the Melba on South Grand, and the Palm on Union Boulevard) and of the huge movie palaces downtown and Midtown (like the Ambassador, the St. Louis Theatre, and the Fabulous Fox). Designed with rental spaces for medical, legal, and insurance offices on the upper floors of the movie house buildings, the movie theater buildings from the 1920s and 1930s were designed to make money night and day.

Movies got sound in 1927 with Al Jolson's *The Jazz Singer*. During the Great Depression, the movie houses gave away free pink or green glass dishes (later called "Depression glass") with a double feature. During World War II, factory workers and

*During the Great Depression, neighbors could lift their spirits by seeing the 1937 screen comedies* Fifty Roads to Town *starring Don Ameche and* Call It A Day *with Olivia de Havilland, both showing at the Hi-Pointe. (Photo courtesy of the Missouri Historical Society.)*

soldiers on leave with their dates packed the movie houses. Afterward, color and CinemaScope filled the big screens with Westerns filmed amongst the buttes of Monument Valley. Later, however, the movie houses could not compete with the convenience offered by television. They slowly emptied and were closed. Many of the old movie houses were razed, while others were used as warehouses, churches, and even a drugstore.

Meanwhile, the Hi-Pointe Theater kept showing Hollywood's productions on the big screen. Just as in stage shows, curtains opened at the beginning of each movie feature to reveal the Hi-Pointe's expansive screen. After the movie studios were ordered to sell their movie houses in the 1950s, the local Arthur Enterprises chain operated the Hi-Pointe.

A 1963 remodel gave the Hi-Pointe's interior streamlined, mid-century modern details. Today that *Mad Men* look combined with the theater's neon-lighted marquee announces that this movie house is a unique piece of cinema history.

Though a small, adjacent building now provides an intimate setting for a second screen, the original theater remains unaltered—with one large screen presenting the classic movie house experience.

---

*The son of German immigrants, South St. Louis architect August Foell, along with William Schlesinger, are credited with designing the classic Hi-Point Theatre. Foell designed numerous homes in South City's German neighborhoods, and Schlesinger designed the old Rio Theatre, which opened in the Walnut Park neighborhood of North City in 1939.*

---

# Oldest Track & Field Venue
## Francis Field
Washington University

Francis Field fills the northeast corner of Big Bend and Forsyth Boulevard with track and field facilities for Washington University. It was developed, however, as a venue for the 1904 Olympic track and field competitions that were held in St. Louis in conjunction with the World's Fair. Its formal entrance—a gateway featuring four red granite piers with gray stone quoins and topped by an ornamental iron arch—faces a campus roadway named Olympian Way.

Construction of Francis Field began in 1902 in preparation for the third Olympics in the modern era. Though athletes from 12 countries officially took part in the 1904 Olympics, the first games ever held in the Western Hemisphere, it was truly an amateur athletic competition. *Post-Dispatch* reporter John McGuire

*The gate to Francis Field was constructed in 1914 with proceeds from the 1904 World's Fair. (Photo by NiNi Harris.)*

decades later stated that the Olympic Games "had all the pizzazz of a church picnic or a pickup ball game on a vacant lot."[62]

After the Olympics, Washington University began using the field and stadium for football, track and field, and other athletic competitions. In the first gridiron game at the field, held in September 1905, the Wash U Bears walloped Westminster College 59-0.

A couple years later, the field was named Francis Field in honor of the grain dealer turned politician and civic leader, the persuasive David R. Francis. As president of the Louisiana Purchase Exposition, he had maneuvered the Olympic Games to St. Louis.

The stadium, with seating for 19,000, often hosted a highlight of the St. Louis sports scene. From the early years of the 20th century until World War II, the annual Thanksgiving Day football game between Washington University and Saint Louis University filled the stands with alumni.

Though Francis Field underwent significant renovations in 1984, reducing the seating to 3,300, Washington University athletes still compete on the field where Olympic gold was won in 1904.

---

*Thomas Kiely, who was listed as from Ireland, won the all-around Olympic championship for field events, which included 10 contests held in one day on Francis Field. Since Ireland was still ruled by England, Kiely officially competed for England.*

---

# ENDNOTES

1   John Caspar Wild, *Valley of the Mississippi, Illustrated*, Chambers & Knapp, Printers, Publisher at the Republican Printing Office, Main Street, St. Louis. 1841. p. 17.

2   *Old Courthouse*, National Park Service brochure, c 1970.

3   *St. Louis Business Journal*, "William H. Danforth's daring spirit nourished Ralston Purina." September 5-11, 1994.

4   *St. Louis Post-Dispatch*. "A Checkered Past." September 25, 1994, p. 1f.

5   The Commerce Department issued a license to the Pulitzer company to operate KSD days before WEW received its license. Its place on the dial, 550 AM, has been home to KTRS since 1997.

6   Sullivan, Louis H. *Kindergarten Chats and Other Writings*. New York: George Wittenborn, 1947, p. 206.

7   Welcome to The First Baptist church of St. Louis and Its Ministries, "A Church With A Purpose." *First Steps at First Baptist*. The directory includes a history of the congregation. Appears to have been published in 2017.

8   *St. Louis Post-Dispatch*. "Firemen Fight Church Blaze in Sub-Zero Cold." January 18, 1940.

9   The census records and city directories had a variety of spellings for the name Karandzieff.

10  January 17, 2008, *KETC, Living St. Louis*, "Crown Candy."

11  Peck, John Mason. *Father Clark, or The Pioneer Preacher: Sketches and Incidents of Rev. John Clark by an Old Pioneer*. New York: Sheldon, Lamport & Blakeman, 1855, p. 285.

12  Ibid.

13  The oldest public golf course in operation west of the Mississippi is the Normandie Golf Club, built in 1901. The Log Cabin Club was founded in 1899, then bought their property in Ladue and established a golf course with only nine holes.

14  Following the games in St. Louis, golf was dropped from the Olympics until 2016.

15  Stille, Ron. Interview by the author, NiNi Harris, May 31, 2020.

16  Ibid.

17  Moore, Ruth, "A tour of the neighborhood gardens." *St. Louis Star and Times*. July 2, 1935.

18  Ibid.

19  Though always affectionately known as Florissant, during much of its early history, Florissant's official name was St. Ferdinand.

20  A brochure published for St. Louis bicentennial in 1964 by the Florissant Bicentennial of St. Louis Committee.

21 Hahn, Valerie S. "100: Gus' Pretzels." *St. Louis Post-Dispatch.* January 10, 2020.

22 Ibid.

23 Schmidt, Kurt. Interview by the author, April 10, 2020.

24 Ibid.

25 Spanish colonial-era legal documents, translated in the 1840s, transcribed as part of a WPA project during the 1930s, in the collections of the Old Courthouse.

26 Blassie's remains were buried in the Tomb of the Unknowns at Arlington National Cemetery in 1984. After his mother succeeded in having the remains tested, DNA results revealed they were those of Lieutenant Blassie. In 1998, the remains were reburied at Jefferson Barracks.

27 Sigman, Leroy. "Headstones mark resting place of nation's heroes." *Daily Journal Online.* May 30, 2004. https://dailyjournalonline.com/news/local/headstones-mark-resting-place-of-nations-heroes/article_dbd9eb6d-b860-54b9-9bf9-160cffc6aca4.html.

28 The A.M.E. Church was organized in 1816 by African American churches in the east. They accepted Methodist teachings. They used the word Episcopal because their highest officer in the church was a bishop.

29 Early records of these congregations are believed to have burned along with the brick church in 1869.

30 National Register nomination for Quinn Chapel, A.M.E. Church, dated July 20, 1974.

31 Ibid. Sec. 8 #1.

32 Census entries and city directories from 1870 through 1920.

33 Obituary of Clarence Winkelmann, *St. Louis Post-Dispatch*, January 28, 1976.

34 The author has done a study of the earliest construction in the Carondelet neighborhood, based on fieldwork and on Spanish colonial documents. Some of the results of her study are on exhibit at the Carondelet Historical Society.

35 *St. Louis Post-Dispatch.* "Giver approves library plans," June 21, 1903.

36 *St. Louis Post-Dispatch*, "New library is busy," September 26, 1906.

37 *St. Louis Post-Dispatch.* Archibald, John J., "30 Years At McDonald's," D.1.

38 Ibid.

39 *St. Louis Post-Dispatch.* "Famous-Barr Plans $10,000,000 Lemay Center in South County." March 15, 1961.

40 Letter from Hooker to Shaw dated Aug. 10, 1857, in Scrapbook I to 1890.

41 As a child attending nature classes at the garden, the author saw displays of insects in the museum.

42 Stevens, Walter B.; Byars, William Vincent. *St. Louis in the Twentieth Century: A Hundred Years of Progress Illustrated by Over Two Hundred Views.* St. Louis: Woodward & Tiernan, 1909.

43 Greg Houston interview June 16, 2020.

44  Ibid.

45  After the Schmitzes were operating the spice shop in Soulard Market, they continued operating the grocery on 9th Street until 1987.

46  Fremont, Jessie Benton. *Souvenirs of My Time*. Boston: Lothrop & Co, 1887. pp. 168–172.

47  William B. Faherty, S.J., *Better the Dream, Saint Louis: University & Community 1818–1968*, St. Louis: St. Louis University, 1968. p. 8.

48  Ohmeyer, Ada. Interviews with the author. Mid-1980s.

49  Hahn, Valerie Schremp. "Saratoga Lanes in Maplewood, the area's last upstairs bowling alley, celebrates 100 years." *St. Louis Post-Dispatch*. October 7, 2016,

50  "Billy" Busch, son of August A. Busch, Jr. and Trudy Busch, bought the Bridle Spur property in St. Charles County.

51  *St. Louis-Post-Dispatch*. "Rabbis Dedicate New Temple Israel." September 8, 1962.

52  Though many older buildings constructed as Jewish houses of worship dot the city and county, they have not served Jewish congregations for years.

53  *St. Louis Post-Dispatch*. "Temple Israel to Celebrate Its 70th Anniversary Tonight." December 7, 1956.

54  Stiritz, MiMi. *St. Louis Historic Churches & Synagogues*. St. Louis: St. Louis Public Library and Landmarks Association of St. Louis, 1995. p. 81.

55  An agency that verifies that products meet the requirements of Jewish laws pertaining to food.

56  *St. Louis Post-Dispatch*. "Bagels not so lonely in kosher case." September 16, 1985.

57  McCue, George. "The New Church Architecture, Congregations Increasingly Receptive to Contemporary Style." *St. Louis Post-Dispatch*, February 17, 1957.

58  U. City Shul website (www.ucityshul.org).

59  Silver Anniversary Souvenir 1943, St. Louis Municipal Opera, The Significance of the St. Louis Municipal Opera as interpreted by its longtime president, the late Henry W. Kiel.

60  Ibid.

61  Ibid.

62  *St. Louis Post-Dispatch*. "St. Louis' Homegrown Olympic Games." July 22, 1984.

# SOURCES

**Oldest Church**

Wild, John Caspar. *Valley of the Mississippi, Illustrated*. St. Louis: Chambers & Knapp, Printers, 1841. pp. 17–19.

Oestreich, Kenneth D.; Wayman, Norbury L. *St. Louis Landmarks: A Guide to the City's Landmarks and Historic Districts*. St. Louis Community Development Agency, July 29, 1977.

**Oldest Concert Hall**

The State Historical Society of Missouri.

S0361 Ethical Society (1886- ) Of St. Louis Tapes, 1952-1986. 73 Reels, 134 Cassettes.

**Oldest House Garden**

Photos and land records from the Robert Campbell House Museum papers.

**Oldest Hotel**

Nomination for National Register of Historic Places.

Walsh, Marty. Interview by the Author, 1999.

**Oldest Murals**

National Endowment for the Arts; Missouri Arts Council. "Five St. Louis Artists, Their City and Their World." Exhibition hosted by the Missouri Historical Society. 1984.

Tillinger, Elaine. "St. Louis Artists in the Henry Shaw Era" Lecture, March 1, 1991. Tower Grove Lecture series.

US Works Projects Administration Writers' Program. *Missouri: A Guide to the "Show Me" State*. New York: Duell, Sloan & Pierce, 1941.

**Oldest Pet Food**

Faherty, William B. *The Saint Louis Portrait*. Tulsa, OK: Continental Heritage, 1978.

*St. Louis Post-Dispatch*, "Purina's 'Chow' Legends Offer Food for Thought," September 25, 1994, p. 10f.

Fisher, Max. Spirit of Purina Mills 1894-1994, Purina Mills, Inc., 1994.

**Oldest Radio Station**

Waide, John. *Brother George Rueppel, S.J.: The Father of St. Louis radio*. Manuscript completed 2020, Pius the XII Library, St. Louis University.

Faherty, William B., S.J. *Better the Dream, Saint Louis: University & Community 1818–1968*. St. Louis: St. Louis University Press, 1968.

Anonymous. "WEW celebrates twelfth year of broadcasting." *Radio and Entertainment*, May 6, 1933. Courtesy of the St. Louis Media History Foundation.

Anonymous. "WEW was definitely the first." St. Louis Journalism Review. March, 2001. Courtesy of the St. Louis Media History Foundation.

**Oldest Theatre Organ**
St. Louis Theatre Organ Society. *The Fox 4-36 Organ*. (2007).

St. Louis Theatre Organ Society. *Saint Louis Fox Theatre, 1929*. (2007).

*Senior Circuit*, December, 1998, "Stan Kann Returns."
US Department of the Interior. National Park Service. National Register of Historic Places Inventory Nomination Form. Washington, DC, 1975.

**Oldest University**
Faherty, William B., S.J. *Better the Dream, Saint Louis: University & Community 1818–1968*. St. Louis: St. Louis University Press, 1968.

Hill, Walter H., S. J. *Historical Sketch of the St. Louis University; the Celebration of its Fiftieth Anniversary or Golden Jubilee, on June 24, 1879*. St. Louis: Patrick Fox, 1879.

**Oldest African American Congregation**
Wilbon, Roderick. "First Baptist Church of St. Louis, oldest African-American church west of the Mississippi River, celebrates its 200th anniversary." *St. Louis American*, April 28, 2017.

Jacobs, Robert P., ed. *Religions in St. Louis: A Strong Heritage*. St. Louis: Interfaith Clergy Council, 1976.

**Oldest Ice Cream Parlor & Candy Shop**
1920 census.

Rygelski, Jim. "Crown stays king in North St. Louis." *North Side Journal*. November 12, 1997.

Pollack, Joe. "Crown Candy Kitchen is visit to the good old days." *St. Louis Post-Dispatch*. January 19, 1988.

*St. Louis Post-Dispatch*. "Ice cream of homemade variety." August 29, 1972.

*St. Louis Post-Dispatch*. "How sweet it is: Crown Candy reopening." January 30, 1984.

**Oldest Church Graveyard**
Historic Places Registration Form for Cold Water Creek Cemetery, dated April 7, 2004.

**Oldest Drive-In Curb-Service Restaurant**
Obituary of Ralph Stille. *St. Louis Post-Dispatch*. November 21, 1999.

Rothbarth, Adam. "The last Chuck-A-Burger drive-in sticks to the classics in St. John." *Sauce*. July 9, 2019.

*St. Louis Post-Dispatch*. "Ordinances, fees, guards used to cope with drive-in rowdyism." June 25, 1969.

*Suburban Journals*. "St. John: Still cruisin': Chuck-A-Burger will stay open." March 26, 2008.

**Oldest Fish Market**
Holleman, Joe. "Spotlight: Kram Fish Co.—All that remains of old St. Louis Jewish neighborhood." *St. Louis Post-Dispatch*. December 1, 2015.

Kram, Ed. Interview by the author, May 18, 2011.

## Oldest Hardware Store

Census records from 1870 to 1920.

City directories from 1872 to 1900.

Copy of passport for "Friedrich Marx," issued March 4, 1848, in Hummersen, Germany.

Marx, Steve. Interview by the author, April 9, 2020.

Rombauer, Robert J. *The Union Cause in St. Louis in 1861: An Historical Sketch*. St. Louis: Nixon-Jones, 1909.

## Oldest Brick House

Oestreich, Kenneth D.; Wayman, Norbury L. *St. Louis Landmarks: A Guide to the City's Landmarks and Historic Districts*. St. Louis Community Development Agency, July 29, 1977.

Scharf, Thomas J. *History of Saint Louis City and County, from the Earliest Periods to the Present Day: Including Biographical Sketches of Representative Men*. Philadelphia: Louis H. Everts & Co., 1883.

## Oldest House in St. Louis County

St. Louis County Department of Parks and Recreation. *The Past in Our Presence: Historic Buildings in St. Louis County*. Clayton, Missouri: St. Louis County Department of Parks and Recreation, 1996.

St. Louis County Historic Buildings Commission; St. Louis County Department of Parks and Recreation; St. Louis County Department of Human Resources. *Historic Buildings in St. Louis County*. 2nd ed. Clayton, Missouri: St. Louis County, 1985.

US Department of the Interior, National Park Service. *National Register of Historic Places Inventory Nomination Form*. Washington, DC: US Department of the Interior, 1976.

## Oldest Public Housing

Oestreich, Kenneth D.; Wayman, Norbury L. *St. Louis Landmarks: A Guide to the City's Landmarks and Historic Districts*. St. Louis Community Development Agency, July 29, 1977.

*St. Louis Star and Times*. "Civic leaders to join in low cost home ceremony." May 22, 1934.

March 15, 1934 clipping—publication not shown (Collections of SLPL).

*St. Louis Post-Dispatch*, July 14, 1935, clipping (Collections of SLPL).

*St. Louis Post-Dispatch*, Wednesday, March 14, 1934, clipping (Collections of SLPL).

## Oldest Municipality in St. Louis County

McDermott, John Francis, ed. *The Early Histories of St. Louis*. St. Louis: St. Louis Historical Documents Foundation, 1952.

*Progress in Historic Preservation*, East-West Gateway Coordinating Council, St. Louis (Illinois-Missouri) Metropolitan Area, prepared by Mrs. Leslie Davison, Historic Florissant, Inc., April, 1978.

Scharf, Thomas J. *History of Saint Louis City and County, from the Earliest Periods to the Present Day: Including Biographical Sketches of Representative Men*. Philadelphia: Louis H. Everts & Co., 1883.

St. Louis County Department of Parks and Recreation. *The Past in Our Presence: Historic Buildings in St. Louis County*. Clayton, Missouri: St. Louis County Department of Parks and Recreation, 1996.

**Oldest Polish Sausage Shop**
Census records and city directories.
Harris, NiNi, *Unyielding Spirit, the history of the Polish people in St. Louis*, St. Stanislaus Kostka Parish, St. Louis, Mo., 2007.

**Oldest Vigil**
Census record and city directories: 1880–1920.
*In the Shadow of the Sanctuary, Sisters, Servants of the Holy Ghost of Perpetual Adoration*, Imprimatur September 17, 1931.
*A Message from Mount Grace Convent of Perpetual Adoration*, Imprimatur Oct. 7, 1936.
*Saint Louis Foundation Mount Grace Convent and Chapel of Perpetual Adoration*. September, 1974.
*St. Louis Globe-Democrat* (Sunday Magazine). "The cloistered world of the Pink Sisters." June 25, 1978.
*St. Louis Post-Dispatch* (Everyday Magazine). "Marking 40 years in St. Louis." June 7, 1968.
*St. Louis Post-Dispatch*. "Three describe witnessing will of Mrs. Kulage." May 15, 1935.

**Oldest Cookie Bakery**
Hastey, Ken. Interview by the author, March 16, 2020.
Street numbering certificate for 3854 Louisiana.
Federal census records for 1920, 1930, and 1940.

**Oldest Pretzel Factory**
Berger, Eric. "Gus' Pretzels hits 100 years of hand-twisted goodness," *Alive*. March 1, 2020.
Census records from 1910 to 1940.
Koebbe, Gus Jr. Interview by the author, May 5, 2020.

**Oldest Ballroom**
City directories.
Glaus, Heidi. "Casa Loma Ballroom celebrates 90 years. Published March 16, 2017, www.ksdk.com.
Keaggy, Diane. "A bygone era lives on at 85-year-old Casa Loma Ballroom." *St. Louis Post-Dispatch*. September 6, 2012.
Lossos, David A. *Images of America: St. Louis Casa Loma Ballroom*. Mount Pleasant, SC: Arcadia, 2005.
*St. Louis Post-Dispatch*. "$150,000 Building for South Side." August 4, 1940.

**Oldest Billiards Table Manufacturer**
City directories and census records from 1860 to 1900.

**Oldest Bohemian Landmark**
Harris, NiNi. *Bohemian Hill: An American Experience*. St. Louis: St. John Nepomuk Parish, 2004.

### Oldest Cemetery

Fusco, Tony. *The Story of Jefferson Barracks National Cemetery*, St. Louis: published by Tony Fusco, 1967.

News clippings collections about Jefferson Barracks and the National Cemetery assembled by Tony Fusco in the Carondelet Historical Society collections.

Snyder, Edwin Pfc. *A Grand Old Post: Jefferson Barracks—A Brief Historical Account Prepared For Distribution to the Personnel, Jefferson Barracks, MO.* 1945. In Carondelet Historical Society collections.

(Prepared by the Aeronautical Chart Service, Photogrammetry Unit, Army Air Forces.)

### Oldest African American Church Building

"We've Come This Far by Faith" Quinn chapel, African Methodist Episcopal Church, 141st Anniversary, June 8, 1986. Including a congregation history by Charles U. Brown, Sr.

"Reflections of Carondelet," 1891-1966, published by Southern Commercial and Savings Bank.

St. Louis Commercial Directories, or Red Books from the 1880s.

### Oldest Convent

Carondelet Consolidated Archive of the Sisters of the St. Joseph of Carondelet.

Savage, Sister Mary Lucida. *The Congregation of Saint Joseph of Carondelet, A Brief Account of Its Origin and Its Work In The United States (1650–1922)*, 2nd ed. St. Louis: B. Herder Book Co., 1927.

Website of the Sisters of St. Joseph of Carondelet, St. Louis Province, https://www.csjsl.org/motherhouse.

### Oldest Drugstore

Building permits issued by the City of St. Louis for structures at the intersection of Meramec St. and Virginia Ave.

Dickson, Terry. "He's spent 64 years in drug business: Henry Winkelmann has owned store in South St. Louis for 50 years." *St. Louis Post-Dispatch*. October 20, 1952.

*St. Louis Post-Dispatch*. "14th in family enters college of pharmacy." September 13, 1962.

*St. Louis Post-Dispatch*. "Drugstore closing after 112 years." June 11, 1972.

*St. Louis Post-Dispatch*. "Ernst A. Winkelmann Dies, drug firm head." February 19, 1952.

### Oldest Florist

City directories and census records from 1870 to 1910.

Knoll, Chuck. Interview by the author, May 20, 2020.

Kruse, Denise. "It's all relative: Walter Knoll Florist." *Ladue News*. April 23, 2015.

Obituary of W.R. Knoll. *St. Louis Post-Dispatch*, Feb. 29, 1960.

Tighe, Theresa. "Floral companies are keeping their roots in St. Louis' Florists' Row." *St. Louis Post-Dispatch (South Post)*. November 17, 2003.

Whippel Fire Insurance Map of 1895.

## Oldest Greenhouse

Barnett, Tom P. "George I. Barnett, pioneer architect of the West." *Western Architect.*

"Chronological history of the early days of Shaw's Garden." *Missouri Botanical Garden Bulletin*, 1950 (March) Vol. XXXVIII, No. 3.

Faherty, William Barnaby S.J. *Henry Shaw: His Life and Legacies*, University of Missouri Press, Columbia, 1987.

## Oldest Library Building

*St. Louis Post-Dispatch.* "Barr Branch dedicated: Joint gift of St. Louis merchant and Carnegie." Sept. 16, 1906, p. B7.

*St. Louis Post-Dispatch.* "The new branch libraries: figures which show how the reading habit is spreading in St. Louis." September 13, 1908, p. B10.

St. Louis Public Library newsletter, September 9, 2016.

## Oldest *Mad Men* Firm

Christopher Haller, Executive Vice President and Owner of Obata. Interview with the author. May 27, 2020.

## Oldest Shopping Mall

*South Side Journal.* "Sears, shops open at South County Mall." October 28, 2001.

*St. Louis Globe-Democrat.* "Grand opening today, South County Center Plans three day celebration." October 17, 1963.

*St. Louis Globe-Democrat.* "Shimmering curtain of raindrops." August 8, 1963.

*St. Louis Post-Dispatch.* "Multi-million dollar expansion planned for South County Mall." June 23, 1978.

## Oldest Public Market

Billon, Frederic L. *Annals of St. Louis in its Early Days under the French and Spanish Dominations*, Printed for the Author. St. Louis, 1886.

*The Messenger* (The St. John Nepomuk Parish monthly magazine). August 1929, "The Name of Soulard Has Been Inseparably Linked With the Growth of St. Louis Since 1794." p. 4 article based on material shared with the congregation during Henry G. Soulard's decades-long membership in St. John Nepomuk Parish.

MS. *A Brief History of the Public Markets and Private Markets Referred to as Public Markets in the City of St. Louis Missouri from the Time of Their Inception in 1764 thru the Present Date* as compiled by Philip Taylor, Market Master, City of St. Louis, January 1961.

## Oldest Museum

Anonymous. "Chronological History of the Early Days of Shaw's Garden." *Missouri Botanical Garden Bulletin 38* (3), 1950.

Faherty, William Barnaby. S.J., *Henry Shaw: His Life and Legacies.* Columbia, MO: University of Missouri Press 1987.

US Work Projects Administration. *The WPA Guide to 1930s Missouri.* New York: Duell, Sloan and Pearce, 1941. Reprint, Lawrence, KS: Kansas University Press, 1986.

**Oldest Park**

Darby, John F. *Personal Recollections of John F. Darby, Mayor of St. Louis, 1835, Sketches of Prominent People and of Events Relating to the History of St. Louis During the First Half of the Nineteenth Century.* St. Louis: G.I. Jones and Company, 1880. p. 156.

Matthews, Leonard. *A Long Life in Review, Autobiographical Notes.* Self-published, 1928.

**Oldest Private Place**

Bryan, John Albury. *Lafayette Square: The Most Historical Neighborhood in St. Louis.* Landmarks Association of St. Louis, 1969.

Compton & Dry, *Pictorial St. Louis,* 1875.

**Oldest Spice Shop**

Census records and city directories from 1910 to 1940.

Schmitz, Linda. Interview by the author, May 7, 2020.

**Oldest Statue**

The editorial staff of The Mentor Association Illustration for the Mentor Vol. 6 No. 24, Serial No. 172, 1919.

Scharf, Thomas J. *History of Saint Louis City and County, from the Earliest Periods to the Present Day: Including Biographical Sketches of Representative Men.* Philadelphia: Louis H. Everts & Co. 1883.

**Oldest Commercial Street**

City directories 1930–1970.

Klingl, Joe. Interview by the author, February 15, 1977.

Thomann, Pat. Interview by the author, April, 28, 2020.

**Oldest Billiards Hall**

*St. Louis-Post-Dispatch.* "$130,000 for school from Backer estate." October 24, 1936.

*St. Louis-Post-Dispatch.* "Work to begin at once." June 11, 1922.

**Oldest Bowling Alley**

1900 Census Compendium

Powell, William. "Saratoga lanes turns 100: The classic bowling alley in Maplewood celebrates its centennial." *St. Louis Magazine.* February 18, 2016.

United States Department of the Interior, National Park Service. *National Register of Historic Places Registration Form,* 2007.

**Oldest Coffee Roaster**

City directories beginning in 1854.

Leonard, Mary Delach. "Coffee high: Local entrepreneur works to bring back Thomas Coffee—and city's coffee district." KWMU Public Radio, St. Louis, August 11, 2010.

Missouri Historical Society. "Coffee: The World in Your Cup & St. Louis in Your Cup." Exhibit, October 3, 2015 to January 3, 2016.

Merrilees, Annika, *St. Louis Post-Dispatch*. "Brewing Growth." July 28, 2019.

Kumar, Kavita, *St. Louis Post-Dispatch*, "Ronnoco Coffee furthers expansion with Love Bottling Co. in Oklahoma," February 4, 2014.

**Oldest Hospital Building**
https://www.barnesjewish.org/About-Us/History, Barnes/Jewish Hospital website.

https://obgyn.wustl.edu/about/history, Washington University School of Medicine. Department of Obstetrics and Gynecology. Website.

**Oldest Hunt Club**
Herndon, Peter; Ganey, Terry. *Under the Influence: The Unauthorized Story of the Anheuser-Busch Dynasty*. New York: Simon & Shuster, 1991.

Vandewater, Judith. "Fox Hunt Club Enjoying Fruits of Endurance." *St. Louis Post-Dispatch (St. Charles Post)*. June 21, 1994.

**Oldest Reform Jewish House of Worship**
Anonymous. "Rabbi Leon Harrison of St. Louis." *American Jewess* 5(1), 15–16, 1897.

*St. Louis-Post-Dispatch*. "Temple Israel to Celebrate Its 70th Anniversary Tonight," December 7, 1956.

*St. Louis-Post-Dispatch*. "House of worship in campus-like setting." January 25, 1959.

*St. Louis-Post-Dispatch*. "Rabbi Issermann: Always on 'side of the angels.'" February 21, 1963.

*St. Louis-Post-Dispatch*. "Rabbis dedicate new Temple Israel." September 8, 1962.

**Oldest Kosher Butcher and Deli**
Obituary of Simon Kohn. *St. Louis Post-Dispatch*, July 4, 2013.

Obituary of Simon Kohn. *Jewish Light,* July 5, 2013.

**Oldest Skating Rink**
Anonymous. "Behind the building: Frederick Dunn, the gentleman architect." *St. Louis Magazine*, August 22, 2011.

Loughlin, Caroline; Anderson, Catherine. *Forest Park*. Columbia, MO: Junior League of St. Louis and University of Missouri Press, 1986.

**Oldest Jewish House of Worship**
Census records for 1910, 1920, and 1930.

Historic Buildings Survey, Art Deco & the International Style, St. Louis and St. Louis County, Missouri, 1987, prepared by Esley Hamilton.

**Oldest Family-Owned Tavern**
Census records.

Failoni, Joey. Interview by the author, June 20, 2020.

Obituary of Joseph Frank Failoni. *St. Louis Post-Dispatch*, August 10, 2006.

**Oldest Irish Pub**

Jovanovich, Joe. Interview by the author, July 8, 2020.

**Oldest Italian Tavern**

Census records for 1910, 1920, 1930, and 1940.

City directories from 1920 to 1940.

Obituary for Louis Merlo. *St. Louis Post-Dispatch*, December 14, 1948.

Street Numbering Certificate issued by the St. Louis Street Department dated Oct. 17, 1905.

Venegoni, George. "Merlo's Tavern." The Hill newsletter, 2000.

# INDEX